The Beginner's Vegetable Garden 2021:

The Complete Beginners Guide To Vegetable Gardening in 2021

Leslie Martin

TABLE OF CONTENTS

THE BEGINNER'S VEGETABLE GARDEN 2021..1

INTRODUCTION 1

CHAPTER 1 *RAISED BED GARDENING*..3

BASICS 5

    Sun...6

    Drainage..6

    Water 7

    Logistics..9

    Size 10

BUILDING STRUCTURES 12

    Materials Needed...13

    Optional...13

    Process 13

    Various Structures 14

    Garden Covers 15

PLANTS 16

    Plant Journal 16

    Understanding the Plant Needs 17

    Spacing..17

    Companion Planting...18

    Plants for Repelling Diseases and Pests 18

    Combination for Improving Flavor 19

    Best Combination for Raised Bed Garden 20

CROP ROTATION..20

Reason for Crop Rotation 21

Crop Rotation Principles 21

Challenges for Raised Bed Crop Rotation 21

Sample Plan for Planting 22

Supplementing Garden Beds 22

Tips For Effective Crop Rotation 22

SOIL 23

How Much Soil Is Required? 24

Best Soil for Raised Bed 25

Amending Soil Mixture 25

Maintenance 26

PLANTING 27

Seeds 27

Where to Sow Seeds? 27

PROCESS OF SOWING SEEDS 28

Planting Seedlings 29

Planting Seeds in Block 29

GROWING AND HARVESTING 30

Watering 30

Paying Attention to Weather 30

Being Aware of the Watering Needs 30

Water During Morning 31

Thinning and Feeding Seedlings 31

Mulching 31

Fertilizing 32

Harvesting 32

Weeding 32

Pest Control 33

CHAPTER 2 *CONTAINER GARDENING* **35**

Basics 37

 Sun 38

 Drainage 39

 Water 41

 Logistics 43

 Size 43

 Types of Containers 44

Building Structures and Designs 45

 Proportion 46

 Focal Point 46

 Designing With the Help of Edible Plants 46

Plants 47

 Plant Journal 47

 Spacing 47

Plants Suitable for Container Gardening 48

 Beans 48

 Beets 48

 Chard 49

 Peppers 49

 Companion Planting 49

 Salad Mix 49

 Root Vegetables 49

 Tomatoes 50

 Squash and Beans 50

CROP ROTATION...50

    Simple Rotation of Crops..51

    Rotating Crops According to Harvest Groups...51

    Crop Rotation With Plant Family...52

SOIL...53

    Choosing Soil for Potting...53

    Best Soil for Gardening in Containers..54

    Soil for Large Containers...55

    Soil for Hanging Baskets...55

    Reusing Container Soil...55

PLANTING...56

    Sowing Seeds..56

PROCESS OF SOWING SEEDS..57

GROWING AND HARVESTING...59

    Watering..59

    Thinning..61

    Mulching..62

    Fertilizing..62

    Harvesting...63

    Weeding...63

PEST CONTROL...64

PROS & CONS...65

    Pros...65

    Cons...66

CHAPTER 3 *IN-GROUND GARDENING*..**68**

BASICS..70

Sun..70

Drainage...71

Water..71

Logistics..72

Size...73

BUILDING STRUCTURES 75

Materials Needed for Window Frame Trellis 75

PLANTS...76

Plant Journal 76

Spacing...76

COMPANION PLANTING 77

Roses and Garlic...77

Cabbage and Tomato..78

Dill and Cabbage 78

Beans and Corns...78

Spinach and Radish...78

CROP ROTATION...78

Plant Groups for Crop Rotation 79

Crop Rotation and Its Benefits for In-Ground Gardening 80

Planning Crop Rotation 81

SOIL...82

Soil pH 83

Soil Density...83

Mix 84

Maintenance...84

PLANTING..84

Hill Method..85

Trough Method 85

GROWING AND HARVESTING 86

Watering 86

Watering Less and Thoroughly 87

Keep the Leaves Dry 87

Avoid Waterlogging 87

Thinning 87

Mulching 88

Fertilizing 88

Harvesting 88

Weeding 89

PEST CONTROL 90

PROS & CONS 91

Pros 91

Cons 92

CHAPTER 4 *PLANT PROFILES* **94**

BASIL 94

Growing 96

BELL PEPPER 96

Starting 97

Growing 97

CABBAGE 98

Starting 99

Growing 99

BROCCOLI 100

Starting 101

Growing *101*

Beet 102

    Starting *103*

    Growing *103*

Carrot 104

    Starting *105*

    Growing *105*

Cilantro 106

    Starting *107*

    Growing *107*

Chives 107

    Starting *108*

    Growing *108*

Corn 109

    Starting *110*

    Growing *110*

Onion 111

    Starting *112*

    Growing *112*

Gardening Resources 113

CHAPTER 5 *LIST OF COMMON GARDENING TERMS* **114**

CHAPTER 6 *COMPANION PLANTING GUIDE* **119**

Three Sisters 121

Companion Planting Chart 123

CONCLUSION **129**

INTRODUCTION

Congratulations on purchasing *The Beginner's Vegetable Garden 2021,* and thank you for doing so.

The chapters in this book will discuss vegetable gardening and the various ways in which it can be done. If you are a beginner in gardening or just love gardening as your hobby, you should try out vegetable gardening. You will come across various skills in this book that can help you to grow vegetables on your own. The basics of gardening can be found in this book. It might be that the weather where you live is very uncertain, and it makes gardening a tough job. However, in such cases, you can still grow your own vegetables with the use of raised bed gardening, container gardening, and in-ground gardening. All these are the various ways in which you can grow vegetables on your own despite the climate or other factors that might not be in your favor.

Each type of gardening comes with its own set of pros and cons, and I am going to walk you through all of it in this book. With the growing uncertainty of this world along with a rise in world population, growing your own vegetables is turning out to be an essential job. Everything that you need to know for setting up your garden has been included in this book.

There are plenty of books on this subject on the market, thanks again for choosing this one! Every effort was made to ensure it is full of as much useful information as possible, and please enjoy!

CHAPTER 1

Raised Bed Gardening

Some people might think that you need a large yard in order to be able to grow a useful garden. This simply just isn't the case. There are many places all around you that would suffice for you to grow your own garden. Take a look along the edge of the alley or beside the driveway. You can grow vegetables and food everywhere if you can adapt the space properly.

One such adaptation is raised bed gardening. Even when you do not have much time for setting up your garden, you can still have the chance to develop a productive garden of veggies. Not sure how to do that? Don't worry; I am going to explain it all to you. Raised bed gardening can be regarded as the best shortcut for a plentiful harvest. It involves developing raised spaces where you can grow your own plants. You can build your garden anywhere with the help of raised beds. Moreover, you can grow more food in a very confined space. The plants can be placed very close to one another, and each square inch can be made productive.

You can either build your own raised bed or just get one from the market. This will be discussed in the upcoming chapters. But how many raised beds you are required to have for starting? In case you have limited space or time, you can start with one. If you want to increase the vegetable yield with time, you will need more beds. If you are new to the world of gardening, start small. It is always better to get thrilled with all that you can grow in a small-sized garden. Otherwise, it can make you frustrated by the commitment of time that is required by the big ones. Also, it makes more sense to learn the basics of gardening first before you invest your money and time in your hobby. As you start with this, you will soon be getting an idea as to the time that this new endeavor is going to use up from your daily schedule. You will come to know whether you like to spend time watering, planting, and weeding.

A great size for setting up your beginner's garden is 8 x 8 feet. Try keeping it as simple as possible. For starters, do not select more than 3 – 4 types of vegetables. As you start simple, you will be able to get a great amount of produce for summer meals. It will be easier for you to keep up with the gardening chores as well. If you are feeling confused regarding which vegetables to start with, you can start with the ones that you love the most. It can be tomatoes, onions, potatoes, etc. Before you commence, think about the quantity of produce that you want. Try to be realistic about the number of plants or seeds that you will need to reach your target. You can opt for vegetables that can be harvested several times, such as peppers and squash.

If possible, try to opt for both warm and cool weather vegetables. By doing this, you can get a harvest of fresh vegetables continuously through all the seasons. When it is early spring, you can opt for lettuce, peas, broccoli, and carrots. For the hot season, you can plant eggplants, tomatoes, herbs, and peppers. For the cool season, you can plant cabbage, kale, and potatoes. Also, while choosing the spot, try to be thoughtful about the requirements of the garden. Make sure that everything is handy from the spot of your garden. Try to create a checklist that will contain the essentials such as water, sun, drainage, storage, etc. You will also have to ensure that the spot is not prone to insects and pests. The plants will have to be protected from strong winds, heavy rain, and other natural features.

Let us start with the basics of raised bed gardening first, and then we will slowly progress to the other components of the same.

Basics

Just like other types of gardening, raised bed gardening also needs some of the essentials such as sunlight, water, drainage, logistics, etc. You will need to ensure that your garden is getting all that it needs to provide you with the best results.

Sun

Like all other types of plants, vegetables also need enough sunlight to start the process of photosynthesis. Photosynthesis helps in transforming the energy of sunlight into glucose that is used by the plants for making other substances like cellulose and starch. Starch is used as the source of food, while cellulose is needed for building the cellular walls. Vegetables that come with fast-growing speed will need sunlight for about 6 – 8 hours every day. The sunlight needs to be direct without any form of blockage from fences, trees, or shrubs. That is the reason why you might not succeed in your venture of gardening if you plant vegetables that are sun-loving in shady spots.

In case the spot where you have decided to build your garden provides partial shade, try planting veggies and herbs that are suited for such conditions. Vegetables such as chard, kale, lettuce, cilantro, chives, thyme, and parsley do not need much sunlight. Root vegetables such as beet, radish, and carrots might also tend to work if the gardening spot can get at least 4 – 5 hours of direct light from the sun daily. For the fast-growing vegetables, try to set up your raised bed gardening at a place that can get enough sunlight all throughout the day, without shade of any kind. The fast-growing group of vegetables includes cucumber, pepper, tomato, corn, beans, peas, eggplants, etc.

Drainage

Raised bed gardening is sometimes much easier than traditional gardens. Just like the other types of gardening, raised bed gardening also needs proper drainage. It is needed for promoting optimal growth of plants and also for preventing rotting of roots. Having an efficient system of drainage is very important. A well-organized drainage system is when the garden water can drain to the soil bottom, thus preventing water clogging near the root area of the plants. When there is an absence of proper drainage, the plants might not be able to grow properly. Rotting of the roots might occur when excessive water stores up near the root area because of the lack of a proper system of drainage. Without adequate drainage, a plant will tend to die slowly. The best way of preventing this is by having a well-planned system of drainage.

Raised bed garden does not come with a bottom and sits on the ground directly. If you have set up a raised bed garden that is taller or knee-height, you will have some extra number of steps for ensuring proper drainage of the garden. Raised bed garden, which is lower than knee-height, will have drainage from the dirt area beneath the garden bed. So, for avoiding standing water in the garden, you will need to place soil for planting the vegetables on the dirt to ensure perfect drainage. You will also need to use certain materials at the bed bottom for making the setup perfect. Pea rocks, stones, and crushed granite can be used. There is something that you have to make sure while placing any of these materials - it is at least 3 inches in depth or more for raising the bed higher. After you have placed the base rocks, you can place soil on top of it. The rocks as the base will ensure drainage of water while preventing planting soil from becoming compact with time.

Water

Smart watering is the secret to the success of gardening. It works specifically in all those places where the weather is dry and warm. In the first week after germination of the seeds or after transplantation of the seedlings, you will need to water the plants frequently for making them strong. After the plants have grown properly, you will need to provide them with a long drink after every few days in place of small showers every day. The water will be moving in deeper into the plant soil, and that will result in deeper growth of the roots.

With deeper roots, the plants will be able to take in the required amount of nutrients and will be able to stay healthy.

Your watering schedule will depend on several factors, such as the composition of the soil and your climate. Clay soil will tend to dry out much faster when compared to sandy soil. Windy and sunny weather tends to dry out soil faster than cloudy and cool weather. Not sure about watering requirements? Try to feel the soil about 4 – 5 inches down from the surface of the garden. If the soil feels dry, it is time for watering. This needs to be done during the rainy season as well. This is because sometimes rainwater might just run off the growing surface rather than getting soaked in the soil. You can add compost to the soil for improving its ability to supply the plants with the required amount of water.

Adding compost to your garden is like adding up sponges to a surface. Water will run through, but some amount of water will also get soaked in the layer of compost. Also, with the help of compost, you will be able to make soil aerated. Thus it will be able to provide better drainage. Plants take in oxygen with the help of roots and are most likely to drown if the soil remains soggy for many days. During hot weather, plants might tend to wilt because of the heat. But, it is not the indication of being deprived of moisture. As you check the soil, you will get to know the actual story.

If you think that your garden needs more water, there are various options for doing so. You can use a watering wand to deliver more water at a faster rate. In case you are away from the garden for a long period, you can get a water timer. It will help in turning on the soaker hose or sprinkler. In order to keep the growing plants productive and healthy, do not allow the soil to get dried out completely. Also, plants that are water-stressed might tend to get tough and bitter in taste. So, make sure that you determine the schedule of watering properly. Try to prevent yourself from overwatering the plants.

Tip: Try to build the garden near the water source. It will help in easing your task.

Logistics

You will need to look after the logistics to ensure easy and frequent access to the garden. Make sure that you have enough feasibility and space for using a garden cart or wheelbarrow, logistics for putting away and bringing tools along with materials, distance for moving amendments from your vehicle to shade, proximity of irrigation or hand-watering, and patterns of foot traffic to ensure harvesting and maintenance. It is very important to keep paths around the garden. It might reduce the space of the garden. But, without having enough space in the surrounding might make the whole task of gardening a bit tough. Plan the beds of gardening that can fit the size of your body to ensure comfort. Ensure that you can reach one side form the other with ease. You can also test run the garden to be sure that it is functional and also comfortable for you.

While planning out your garden, consider the future problems of pests. It is especially important in those areas where there is a pest population nearby, such as gophers, rats, rabbits, squirrels, etc. Will the location that you have chosen permit you to install fencing or enclosures of wire around the garden to protect the plants from pets or wildlife? Try to avoid slopes. Gardening in a sloped area, especially raised bed gardening, might result in draining out of the soil very quickly. Also, it will make the task of watering and planting tougher. There is no reason for getting hard on your back and muscles. When you decide to opt for organic gardening, it will produce a considerable amount of waste material. So, it would be better for you if you set up the garden bed away from the entrance of your home, sidewalks, pool, and seating area.

Gardening in the front yard is accepted and even encouraged by the authorities in various areas. So, try to consider the growing factors first before opting for a place of gardening. Make sure that you check the regulations of the local authorities to avoid problems of any kind in the near future.

Size

The primary goal of having a raised bed garden is to ease the need of the gardeners to step into the garden. In simple words, the garden needs to be easily accessible from all sides. The perfect size of a raised bed garden will be 4 feet wide for the adults and 3 feet wide for children. The length of the garden bed is not as critical, as much as the width of the bed is. But, keep in mind that excessively long garden beds might turn out to be a hassle for walking around. You might also feel a bit tough to work on a large garden. It is true that the length of a raised bed garden will be determined partly by the materials that are available. But, keep a note that the overall lumber cost will increase if you build the garden bed more than 10 – 12 feet in length.

The higher you can build the garden bed, the more soil you will need. This will ultimately be adding to the labor and cost that are involved in the project. If you plan to build a high garden bed, make sure that it is strong enough from the base to tackle the weight of the soil. There are certain considerations that you will need to keep in mind.

- There are certain vegetables that required at least 8 – 10 inches of soil for thriving. In case the height of the bed is lower than the mentioned size, dig the remaining soil below the surface of the bed.

- In case the raised bed is placed on a hard surface, the minimum height mark of 8 – 10 inches might not be deep enough for certain crops, for example, potatoes.

- To permit wheelchair access, you will need to make the bed at least 24 inches tall.

- You can consider setting up gardening beds of various heights for accommodating gardeners of different sizes.

You should take care of the garden orientation as well. But, it won't be much of a problem if enough space is provided between the gardening beds for access. The tall crop will tend to shade the shorter crops that are behind them if crops of all sizes are planted on the same bed.

You will have to plan from the beginning if you want to get new lumber. Lumber generally comes in sizes of 8-, 10-, and 12-feet lengths. So, you can keep the dimension of the garden beds to multiples of 3 or 2 feet for minimizing the waste. For instance, if you are willing to set up a bed of 3 feet by 6 feet, lumber of 12 feet will be perfect.

If you are starting new, you can proceed with small-sized gardening beds. The thickness of the walls will rely on the type of material you use. It is needed to be completely aware of the individual dimensions of each of the garden beds along with the complete plan layout. For example, concrete blocks that are 8 inches in thickness will be taking up more space and will also need more distance for reaching across. Wooden planks that are thick by one-inch will need vertical support after every 3 – 4 feet. Make sure that the surface on which you set up the bed is completely flat. So, you will need to level the frame at the time of installing. For avoiding an excessive amount of excavation, if the place is sloped, you can install garden beds of the shortest dimension that is perpendicular to the slope, such as stair steps. Also, you can alter the shape of the bed according to your space and need.

Building Structures

Building elevated growing areas for growing vegetables is easier than it actually looks. You are required to decide a couple of things, such as the kind of wood you want to use, the height of the bed, whether you want to use pre-made braces for the corners, and so on. As you divide every segment of your raised bed garden, it will help in simplifying the overall construction process. You can opt for concrete blocks or some other material for the growing bed. But, lumber is always available and is cost-effective too.

In the majority of the cases, cedar is preferred as the perfect wood for building a raised bed. This is because cedar is resistant to rot. You can also opt for redwood in the place of cedar. However, redwood is not as abundant as cedar.

As you start with building your raised bed garden, you will need to first determine the spot. In case you have decided to place the bed in the yard, remove grass from the area where you will be placing the bed. After you are done with removing the grass, try to loosen up the soil a bit with the help of a shovel. This is the preparation stage.

The perfect size of a raised bed for beginners is 3 feet by 6 feet and a depth of 1 foot. However, you can adjust the dimensions of the bed according to your needs. The majority of the raised beds are maximum four feet wide for allowing the gardeners to easily get to the center. The minimum depth for herbs and leafy vegetables is 6 inches and 12 inches for root vegetables. You can also eco-stain or apply oil to the woods for extending the life of the same. You can line the bed bottom with mesh net cloth to prevent burrowing animals and fit copper strips within the top edge of the bed for deterring slugs. You can also install hoops of PVC for supporting the row covers.

Materials Needed

Untreated wooden planks according to the dimensions of the garden (untreated)

3 ½ inches of #14 screws

Optional

Three by 6 feet hardware cloth for the bed bottom

18 feet copper stripping

Two PVC pipes

Tin sheet

Process

- In case you want to stain or oil the wooden boards, try to do this before setting up the system. Provide two days for allowing them to dry.

- On the surface where you want to set up the garden, set out two four by four wooden boards: Lay, one board of 3 feet, two by two on the top. Put two four by four-flush posts at the ends.

- Attach the wooden boards using the 3 ½ inch screws.

- Repeat the same process with the other wooden board. You will need to build two like this. These boards will be the short ends of the garden bed.

- Stand the sides on edge and place the 6 feet long boards of 2 by 6.

- Attach the long boards with the help of screws.

- Move the bed in place and level the surface if required.

- Attach strips of copper through the inside edge of the top of the bed for deterring slugs from getting in. You can line the base with the use of hardware cloth and attach pipes of PVC for supporting the shade clothes or row covers. (Optional)

- For making supports for the row covers, use two long pipes of PVC and attach the same to each long side of the garden bed. Secure the pipes in place with the use of screws. The pipe tubes will act as the hoop holders for the row covers.

- Fill up the bed with soil and make it ready for planting.

Various Structures

Raised beds can be designed in various structures. So, you have complete freedom of designing it the way you want. While talking about odd structures, some gardeners have started using trellis for making their raised beds. A simple nature of trellis made out of bamboo stakes and wire mesh can provide support for all your plants. The tired style of designing beds is the most famous out of all. You can design the bed in a way where the plants will be planted in different tiers or steps. You can make them rounded or flat like stairs. People are now opting for the caged version a lot for protecting the plants from animals and pests of all kinds.

Garden Covers

Also known as row cover or garden fabric, a garden cover is a great tool that can help in improving the quality of your gardening. It can be used in various ways:

- Protect the plants from strong wind and cold
- Prevents the spread of diseases and insects
- Prevent the plants and soil from getting overheated

There are various options available to you while choosing the type of row cover that you want for your garden:

- **All-purpose row cover:** They are made from polypropylene and are capable of transmitting about 75% of the available light. They can help in keeping the heat inside, prevent bugs, and can act as a superb windbreak for protecting the small plants. They can protect the plants from frost damage as well.
- **Summerweight fabric:** They are light in weight and cannot trap in much heat. They are most widely used for protecting plants from insects, birds, and diseases. They can transmit about 80% of the available light. But, they are not suitable for blocking rain or frost.
- **Garden Quilt:** They are thicker than the others and can transmit about 60% of the available light. They are used for extending the season of growing into late fall or early spring. This form of row cover is also used for insulating vegetables.

There are various other options available for row covers. You will need to determine the usage first before you opt for the final one for your raised bed garden.

Plants

If you are new to the world of gardening, it is better to start simple. When you have limited space along with time, you might have the urge to grow as many plants as you can. Every gardener grows eggplant and tomatoes in their raised beds. But, that does not mean you will start with such plants from the very beginning. Such types of plants are rewarding in nature but also need extra attention and care. Try omitting them if you are new and opt for something really simple. You can start with simple herbs like thyme and mint. They need lesser care and water as well. You can slowly level up your garden as you gain expertise in the same.

Plant Journal

No matter what type of plants you grow in your raised bed garden, try to keep a journal for the plants that you have grown. This way, you will be able to track the needs of various types of plants along with the perfect weather of growing them. While maintaining a plant journal, do not forget to mention the location of the plant where you have grown them. In this way, you will be able to track their progress as well.

You should keep a proper record of the plants that you grow in each bed. This will help you to make informed decisions about the types of amendments that the soil will need every time while planting. As each plant comes along with individual needs, you can make a table of the requirements for making your task more manageable. For example, tomatoes like to grow in soil that is rich in calcium. So, before planting other crops in a bed that has been used for growing tomatoes, it is better to treat the bed with calcium.

Understanding the Plant Needs

The primary mistake that is made by most of the beginner growers is misunderstanding the plant's needs. We all know that plants such as peppers and tomatoes need more water, more solar energy, and more nutrients from the soil. Before you start growing plants, try to do some research about the type of plants that you are going to choose. How much sunlight do the growing beds receive during the course of the day? What are the nutrient requirements of the plants? As you answer these questions to yourself before growing plants, you will be able to avoid most of the gardening failures.

Spacing

In a raised bed garden, you will be able to grow plants close to each other when compared to other sectors of gardening. In conventional gardening, the plants are required to be placed at least 3 feet away from each other. This is not the case with raised bed gardening. Always keep a note of the number of plants that you are growing. This is because you will need to harvest them at the right time when they are completely ready. Also, at the time of planting, make sure that you consider the size of the plants. If you are growing tall plants, try to grow them on the northern side of the bed for avoiding casting of shadow on the small-sized plants.

Do not grow plants of various types in one bed. If you are opting for the tier system of growing, you can grow plants of each type in each tier. This will help you to keep the tall plants away from the short plants. It is possible to grow crops of various types in one bed when proper spacing is maintained between the plants in the bed.

Companion Planting

Have you ever come across the phrase 'tomatoes love carrots'? This old saying indicated planting two vegetables that are well-loved together as it can help in improving the yield for both. With the help of companion planting, you can improve the flavor of the produce. There will be less dependency on the chemical-based insecticides and pesticides. As raised bed gardens are efficient, neat, and easy to set up, it can group the plants into a very constrained space. So, choosing the perfect companion for the plants is a very important step for getting the best yield from your crops.

Plants for Repelling Diseases and Pests

There are certain plants that can produce compounds for suppressing the development and growth of other harmful organisms in the garden. Here are some most widely found favorites.

Preferred Crops	Plants For Repelling Pests
Tomatoes	Chives, onions, and garlic can help in preventing the munching pests. Borage helps in repelling tomato hornworms. Asparagus helps in repelling nematodes. Cilantro can be used to prevent spider mites.
Broccoli, Kale, Cabbage	Borage can help in deterring moth caterpillars in cabbages. Garlic can also

	help in preventing various pests with the help of its sulfur compounds. Marigolds help in deterring maggots.
Potatoes	Catnip can be planted with potatoes for repelling Colorado potato beetle.
Carrots	Clover is planted in carrot growing beds for repelling various types of pests like wireworms. Carrot rust fly can be repelled by growing lettuce, tansy, and basil.
Cucumber	Nasturtiums and onions are planted for attracting important insects that can feed on beetles.
Squash	Radishes planted with squash plants can repel various types of insects like squash bugs.

Combination for Improving Flavor

There are various combinations of plants that can be used for improving the flavor of the yield. Let's have a look at them.

- Cilantro or basil planted with tomato
- Chervil planted with radishes
- Chamomile planted with onions

Best Combination for Raised Bed Garden

Onion and garlic planted with tomatoes can help in repelling pests of various types like snails and slugs. Basil grown in the same garden bed of tomatoes can help to improve the flavor of ripe tomatoes. You can plant marigold and radish along with cabbage to control cabbage maggots that tend to attack the roots of cabbage. One of the oldest favorites, called the three sisters, is a combination of squash, corn, and runner beans. Squash can benefit a lot when planted along with beans and corn. Corn also acts as a natural trellis for providing support to the vining beans.

You can plant beets with bush beans and kale. Kale and beans help in adding nutrients to the soil and can be harvested faster than beets. Make sure that you do not plant pole beans with beets as they are not at all compatible with each other. Bean of bush variety is always recommended.

If possible, try to plant flowers in the garden. You can opt for flowers that are edible as they help in improving the flavor of the produce.

Crop Rotation

The overall concept of raised bed gardening is very simple- filling up a frame with soil and then planting crops in the same for years. But, there are certain challenges that are accompanied by the crops in a very restricted area every year. Vegetables, when compared to other types of plants, are more prone to diseases and pests if proper care is not taken.

In case pests get entry to the garden bed once, they can multiply very fast. Crop rotation helps a lot in dealing with pests and also helps in bringing back the soil fertility.

Reason for Crop Rotation

- **Prevention of diseases:** The primary reason behind crop rotation is to prevent the spreading of plant diseases. The disease organisms can easily grow over time and thus result in crop failure. As you rotate crops, it helps in keeping a check on such organisms.

- **Soil fertility:** When you keep on growing crops of one type in the same place for a long time, it can degrade soil fertility. Crop rotation helps in replenishing soil fertility by growing crops of various types.

- **Enhancement of nutrients:** Crop rotation helps in enhancing the nutrient content of the soil.

Crop Rotation Principles

The overall concept related to crop rotation depends on the knowledge of the gardener about the plant families of vegetables. It also includes linked quirks and pests. Crop rotation means not cultivating the same or somewhat related kind of crop in the same place for years. This can help in reducing the building up of insects and disease pathogens. Most of the expert growers suggest a rotation cycle of six to seven years. In theory, a garden needs to have a minimum of six to seven beds. You will need to plant each of the beds with a different type of crop every year until the cycle gets completed.

Challenges for Raised Bed Crop Rotation

Specifically, in the small-scale nature of landscapes, having more garden beds is not at all practical. Crop rotation needs to be approached in a creative way in such a case. For many growers, tomatoes are the only reason for cultivating a garden of vegetables. But, the other members of the nightshade group like potatoes, peppers, and eggplant is not possible to be grown in the exact same place every year without resulting in diseases. Soil replacement is a viable option and is expensive as well.

Sample Plan for Planting

With the use of a proper plan and good keeping of record, you can achieve good rotation of crops with as little as four beds only. With every succeeding year, cultivate crops from one bed to the next that is in line. For instance, in a garden with four beds, the first bed can contain onions and spinach during the springtime, tomatoes during summer, and beans at the time of fall. The second bed can hold cabbage, ornamental corn, and beans at the time of fall. The third frame can contain annual rye as the spring cover crop with peppers in summer and garlic at the time of fall. The fourth can contain peas with sweet corn for summer and turnips for the fall.

Supplementing Garden Beds

In all those spaces where having multiple beds is not at all practical, using large-sized containers for growing one plant at a time is the best option. It is a great way for supplementing diversity of the crops. This can help in maintaining the integrity of the crop rotating schedule. There are various types of plants available that are suited for growing in containers.

Tips For Effective Crop Rotation

- Small-sized gardens can be rotated. You can use four areas for planting garden beds.

- Tomatoes and potatoes are closely related to one another. Both are susceptible to diseases of the same kind. That is the reason gardeners group them together. In case you are facing problems with early blight, you will need to separate the two. Make sure that they are placed away from each other.

- As legumes can help in adding nitrogen to the soil, you can follow them by growing leafy crops that love nitrogen. This can help in reducing the need for nitrogen-based fertilizers.

- Root crops tend to break the soil. So, you can follow the growth of root plants with legumes that can help in adding texture to the soil. Also, legumes can grow very well in the soil of loose structure.

- Some vegetables like cucumbers, lettuce, squash, and melons are not much susceptible to diseases. They can be grown almost anywhere or in any kind of space. But, it will be easier for you to plan the garden by rotating and including everything.

- If you have just started with raised bed gardening, you can rotate crops within the number of beds that you have.

Soil

One of the benefits that you can enjoy while growing vegetables in a raised bed is that you can control the quality of the soil. This aspect is of great advantage for all those gardeners who have clay or hard-packed soil, concerns regarding pollutants, or issues with roots of trees. Good quality soil is always regarded as the foundation of a garden that is of a healthy nature. You will want to ensure that vegetables being set up are ready for success only. So, what kind of soil is best suited for raised beds?

You can set up raised beds of any size, but as a standard, the recommended shape is rectangular with about 3 – 4 feet in width and 6 – 8 feet in length with a height of about 10 – 12 inches. All of these dimensions will allow you as a gardener to reach any spot in the bed to sow, plant, and weed without the need to walk on the bed. This results in another benefit when compared to growing crops following the traditional way. The raised bed soil will remain as it is, friable and loose, instead of being packed tight with time because of footsteps. There is no meaning of disturbing the soil quality without any reason.

How Much Soil Is Required?

Filling up a raised bed will need more amount of soil that you actually think. Delivery of soil will make the maximum sense economically. But, if it does not seem practical from the aspect of logistics, you will have to buy it in bags. You will also need to find an area in the yard from where you can take topsoil. You can opt for the various soil calculators that are available online for determining the amount of soil needed for your raised bed.

In case you have cut out sod underneath in the place where you will be setting up the raised bed, flip them, with the grass side down. This will help in filling the bottom part of the bed. You will find lots of soil attached to the grass, and it will break down with time. So, this indicates you need less amount of soil for filling the raised bed. There is no need to use yard soil only. You can get any kind of soil that you think will meet the needs of the crops. Make sure that the topsoil has the highest composition of organic nutrients and matter. Topsoil is the most important layer for a raised bed.

Best Soil for Raised Bed

The most common mix that you can find in the market is the triple mix. It is a great quality mix that comes with compost, topsoil, and black loam or peat moss. A mixture that comes in the ratio of 50/50 is regarded as the perfect blend of soil for raised bed gardens. In the 50/50 mix, you will find a blend of compost and topsoil only. In case you have decided to purchase soil from outside, make sure that you find out where the soil originates from. Topsoil is most often taken from the lands that are being developed for the new subdivisions. It might have been unused for a long period and thus might be devoid of the important nutrients. If you are buying soil bags, look out for labels such as herb mix, organic, vegetable, or organic soil for flowers and vegetables.

No matter what type of soil you purchase, you will need to ensure that you amend the same with proper compost. The rich organic matter acts as an important component that will be holding all the moisture. It will also provide nutrients for the growth of the plants. Compost acts as a very important component in the soil for raised beds, regardless of the mixture of ingredients that you opt for. You can start by filling the raised beds with about ¾ of the triple mix. Even though it comes with compost in it, you can top-dress the soil with ¼ of compost. In case you do not have a compost pile, you can find various types of composts in the market.

Amending Soil Mixture

Both the triple mix and 50/50 mix comes with the basic types of building blocks that you will need for good quality soil in the raised bed. Once you have got the soil of your choice, you can easily amend the soil composition for suiting specific choices of plants. One of the good additions to create well-balanced organic garden soil is slow-releasing organic fertilizer. If you can add this to the soil two to three times in a year, you can easily boost the quality of the soil.

After you have applied it to the soil, do not forget to add compost or mulch for retaining the soil nutrients and moisture. Some other amendments for the soil are:

- Wood chips, shredded bark, or sawdust breaks down at a slow rate and also helps in improving the soil structure.

- You can use used tea bags and coffee grinds for providing the soil with NPK components.

- Dolomite lime can help in improving the soil alkalinity and also adds calcium and magnesium.

- If you want to make the soil well-drained, gypsum can be added.

Mulch helps in holding the soil moisture and also provides protection to the soil from any kind of damage from the sun rays.

Maintenance

Keep removing debris to prevent the development of pests and diseases. Always check for brown edges, wilting, or yellowing in plants. It might be a sign of pest infestation. In such a case, you can use mild insecticide for the soil. Never forget to check the soil condition after a period of heavy rain. You can use a moisture meter to avoid overwatering of soil. Never forget to remove weeds and stalks from the soil. You can also use a pH meter for checking the pH level of the soil.

Planting

Of course, you will not be growing all your vegetables from seeds. You can also opt for readymade plants from the plant nurseries. No matter which route you opt for, this section will be teaching you the various ways of launching your own raised bed garden.

Seeds

Seeds come with great capabilities of producing incredible bounty from the tiny structures. There are various beginner gardeners who regard the starting of seeds warily. But, in actual, seeds are designed a special way in which they can thrive in various conditions and reproduce as time goes on. All that you need to do is to just help them by providing a bit of care. In case you are not willing to start from the seeds, you can opt for transplants. However, seeds do come with certain benefits. They are cheap and many times free. Also, you can find the seeds for rare veggies easily than finding the transplants of the same.

Where to Sow Seeds?

You have got two options for sowing the seeds: in little pots indoors or in the place where you have set up your garden outdoors. You cannot sow seeds of all types of vegetables indoors. Root crops like beets and carrots cannot be disturbed once they have put down roots in the soil. Seeds need warmth, moisture, light, and also oxygen for germination. For sowing seeds, you can use soil that is light and airy in nature. It will provide the seeds with proper air circulation. Maintaining proper moisture might turn out to be a crucial task in the starting. The aim will be to maintain the soil in a state of sponge-damp. Most seeds can germinate when the temperature is maintained between 65 degrees Fahrenheit and 75 degrees Fahrenheit. After the emergence of the seedlings, you will need to provide them with enough light.

Process of Sowing Seeds

Materials needed:

Seeds

Organic mix of soil

Watering can

Trowel

Procedure:

- Start by moistening the bed soil before you sow the seeds. Make sure that the soil is not wet. It needs to be damp. In case you are willing to sow the seeds in containers, this needs to be followed as well.

- Check the packet of seeds for getting information about how deep the seeds need to be sowed in the soil. As a general rule, you can sow seeds at a depth of approximately twice its diameter. So, large-sized seeds, for example, beans, will be sown much deeper than the seeds of carrots. It is better not to sow the seeds too deep as it might make it tough for the seeds to reach the surface of the soil.

- If you are sowing large seeds, use a pencil or chopstick and a poke a small hole in the soil. Place the seed in the hole and cover the hole with soil. For the seeds of small size, you can just sprinkle them on the soil top and just cover them with a light layer of soil. If you are willing to sow many seeds at one time, create a trench of shallow nature with the trowel edge. You can scatter the seeds or place them along the created trench.

- You will need to follow the spacing guidelines along with the direction that has been provided with the seed packet.

- In case you are sowing more than one type of seed, make sure that you mark the area of the seeds.

- Some seeds can germinate within two to three days, while some might take weeks.

- You will need to keep the soil moist all throughout the period of sprouting and germination.

Planting Seedlings

- If the seedlings have been grown in peat pots, you will need to remove the pots and then place the seedlings in the holes prepared by you.

- If you have grown seedlings in plastic pots, make sure that you scrape the base of the seedling properly along with the soil.

- You will need to plant seedlings at the same depth as they were sowed in the growing pots. If you tend to sow them deeper, the plant might fail to breathe.

Planting Seeds in Block

- Start by outlining the blocks with the help of a shallow trench or furrow.

- Lay down tape measure through the block sides to ensure proper spacing of the seeds.

- Try to maintain a gap of 3 inches.

- Start with 3 inches, followed by 6 inches, and so on for your first row.

- For planting the next section, move the measuring tape 3 inches back. Keep on doing this until you have filled up the block.

- After you are done with this, cover the seeds with the help of soil.

Growing and Harvesting

Growing and harvesting are not much tougher in a raised bed garden. You will need to follow certain tips and suggestions for getting the best out of your raised bed.

Watering

No matter which type of system you choose for watering your garden, you will need to pay proper attention at the time of its operation.

Paying Attention to Weather

Plants will need more water when the conditions are windy and dry. During extreme heat, raised bed gardens might require daily watering. During other times of the year, you can water the garden only 2 – 3 times a week.

Being Aware of the Watering Needs

Make sure that you monitor the signs of stress that might result from under watering of the plants. If you have plants in the garden that are wilting during the afternoon but recovers by the morning are suffering from the stress of heat and not water. You will need to permit the growing plants to develop some tolerance to heat by not watering them excessively. Signs of plant over-watering include rotten roots, soft roots, constant wet soil, and leaf drop.

Water During Morning

Plants tend to absorb moisture in an effective way during the morning. As you water the plants early, it can help in hydrating the plants before the heat of the daytime. Morning plant watering also helps in preventing waterborne pests. It can also deal with diseases of various kinds that might occur in case you water plants at night.

Thinning and Feeding Seedlings

A plant's cotyledon or leaves are the first to develop from the soil. These emerging leaves provide the plant with all the required nutrition until the emergence of true leaves. So, after the appearance of the true leaves, you will need to feed the seedlings every week with a combo of liquid emulsion. In case you want to add a little bit of compost or castings of worms to the mix of seed-starting, this step can be skipped.

During this stage, you will need to make several tough decisions regarding what you want to do with the new seedlings. You will need to keep them free to provide room for breathing. So, you will need to thin out the seedlings, cutting down the weakest one at the level of the soil. Your aim will be to leave one seedling every 3 inches. In case you thin the final space at an early stage, you will end up winding with fewer numbers of plants than you actually intended to.

Mulching

You will need to take care of mulching while growing plants in raised beds. It is very important as it helps in retaining soil moisture, deters weeds, and also helps in regulating soil temperature. You can mulch at layers by using four inches of straw mulch or shredded leaves.

Fertilizing

Timing is the key to effective fertilization of vegetables. Young plants, specifically peppers, and tomatoes might find it tough to adjust to outdoor life. So, if you apply fertilizer at an early stage, the tender plant roots might get burnt. Fertilizers come with varying nutrient composition for the plants. You will need to ensure the requirements of the plants in your garden before opting for a fertilizer.

Harvesting

Harvesting can be done best during the morning. You will need to check the garden plants daily for any kind of issues and also look out for the produce that is ready for harvesting. For example, corn needs to be harvested when the cobs start swelling with the tassels turning brown in color. Harvesting of herbs and leafy vegetables can be done according to your preference. For tomatoes, the perfect time for harvesting will be when the tomatoes are red in color and firm. In case you are willing to grow tomato of some other color, you will need to wait for the same.

Weeding

Weeding is an important part of raised bed gardening. The task of weeding will be easier for you during the morning as the watering or dew can help in making the soil loose. If you break up and loosen the soil regularly, it can discourage the growth of weed. In case weed develops, try to pull them out from the roots as much as you can. You can cover the garden with a layer of plastic mulch or cardboard. It will help in minimizing weed growth between the final harvest and the upcoming season of growing. Also, make sure that you clean the garden by removing dead leaves and decaying debris.

Pest Control

Dealing with the problems of diseases and pests is a natural part of gardening. Well, it might feel really disturbing when pests attack the garden at the time of harvesting or when the plants are growing. Insecticides can be used or dealing with them. But, insecticides can effectively alter the pH level of the soil and can also introduce chemical components to the garden. So, it is better to keep them away as much as you can. There are certain ways in which you can control pests without the use of insecticides.

- Try to maintain healthy soil. A healthy type of soil can help in developing a strong immune system for the plants so that they can fight with diseases and pests. In case you want to use fertilizer of any kind, opt for the organic one.

- Choose plant varieties that are resistant to pests. This is one of the easiest ways of dealing with pests. For instance, the tromboncino variety of squash is more pest-resistant than other varieties of summer squash.

- Try to provide the plants with the required supplies. When the plants are deprived of something, they will tend to get weak and can easily attract pests.

- There are various beneficial insects that can eat away pests. Such insects can be attracted to the garden with the use of pollen and nectar. You can also introduce pest eating bugs like ladybugs and lacewings.

- You can plant strong-scented herbs that can help in deterring pests. This is an easy way of keeping away pests from the garden. Some example of strong-scented plants is garlic, calendula, and coriander.

- Crop rotation can help in dealing with pests. It can also help in managing the fertility of the garden soil. You will need to leave a gap of one to two years before planting crops of the same type in a particular area. It might turn out to be a challenge for small spaces, but if a plant gets infested by pests, try not to grow that type of plant in the same area for the next two to three years.

- You can try out interplanting for dealing with pests. It means growing alternate crops between herbs, vegetables, and flowers. Instead of practicing monocropping, try to alternate the row of veggies with beneficial insect attracting plants and flowers that can repel pests.

- In case you notice pest infestation, try to remove them manually. If a plant gets infested by pests, removing that plant from the garden will be the best option. You can use mild insecticides of organic nature in case the infestation spreads rapidly. You can spray neem oil for keeping away pests.

CHAPTER 2

Container Gardening

Tubs, pots, and half barrels overfilled with vegetables and flowers can easily add appeal to a garden of any kind. But, other than improving the look of a garden, container gardening can serve certain practical purposes as well. Container gardening is a perfect choice for all those people who have no or very little space for gardening. Along with growing flowers, gardeners who are limited to a small yard, balcony, or a little patch of sunlight on the driveway can grow various types of vegetables in containers. Herbs such as chives, thyme, and basil can grow quite happily in containers. Thus they can be set in a little spot outside your kitchen area.

Container gardening adds versatility to gardens of both small and large sizes. As you opt for container gardening, you can add instant colors to the garden and add a focal point for the garden. Either place the containers on a pedestal or the ground, hang them from the porch, or mount them on the windowsill. A container garden can help in improving the look of your house from all possible angles. You can pair matching containers by the sides of the front walk for creating a welcoming décor. Container garden on patio or deck can add ambiance and color to your outdoor area of sitting.

You have the option of using large and single containers for decorating outside. But, you can also consider arranging the containers or pots in groups, both large and small, on terraces, stairways, or in any other place in the garden. Pot clusters can contain a wide variety of your favorite plants, herbs, veggies, and flowers. They can also contain dwarf evergreens and perennials that you would like to try. You can also use hanging baskets and window boxes for adding instant appeal and color to your house.

In most of the cases, plants of only one species are grown in containers. But, you can grow two to three species of plants in large containers. Always keep one thing in mind; it is easier to grow your plants in large-sized containers when compared to the small ones. The main reason behind this is large containers can hold more amount of soil. So, they can stay moist for a longer period. Also, large containers can prevent the rapid fluctuation of temperature. The small baskets are most likely to get dried out, and you will need to water the containers two to three times during very hot weather.

Another thing that you will need to keep in mind is to determine the type of plants that you are willing to grow in the containers. There are various factors that can help you in determining how deep and large the containers need to be. Before you opt for a container, try to consider the shape and size of the root system of the plants that you will be growing. The rate at which the plants grow is another factor that you will need to keep in mind. The rootbound plants that come with the tendency of covering every inch of the available soil dry out faster. They won't be able to grow cells. In case you are willing to grow plants of various types in one container, you will need to use large containers for providing enough root space for the growing plants.

The maximum size of a pot or container will depend on the space that you are having, the plants that will be grown in it, and whether you will be moving the same in the future. Just like other types of gardens, container gardening also needs certain basic elements such as oxygen, water, sun, nutrients, etc. You can make a checklist for ticking off the important requirements of plants as you plan to grow them in containers.

Let us start with the basics of container gardening, and we will progress slowly to the other aspects.

Basics

Plants cannot be grown when certain elements are not present, such as water, nutrients, sunlight, drainage, etc. Container gardening is similar to the other sectors of gardening, and it also needs the basic elements of growing.

Sun

Plants grown in containers need sunlight, but the amount of required sunlight will vary from one plant to the other. Vegetables that are grown for the seeds or fruits, such as peppers, tomatoes, cucumber, and eggplant, requires almost 6 – 8 hours of sunlight that is of direct nature every day. Ideally, this can be from dawn till about 3 pm. The sunlight tends to be the hottest after three in the afternoon till sundown. Leafy vegetables such as lettuce, Swiss chard, cabbage, and spinach can grow in less amount of sunlight. Plants like the culinary herbs and flowering houseplants might come with varying requirements of light.

As you decide to grow plants of a certain kind, make sure that you check the labels of seed packets. This needs to be done to find the ideal requirement of sunlight. You will need to get familiar with the amount of sun that is received by a certain spot of gardening. If possible, you can imagine the altering exposure of sunlight as the plants grow leaves and as the seasons keep in changing. For the productive nature of container gardening, it is better not to combine plants that require a varying amount of sunlight. This needs to be followed if you are growing various containers in one single spot or several plants in one pot or container.

The primary advantage of container gardening that it has over the traditional form of soil gardening is that the containers can be moved. In case you find out that the plants are not at all happy with the amount of sun being received, you can easily pick up the containers and place them in some other spot that comes with better conditions for the plants. If you are new to the world of container gardening, it will be better for you if you opt for the native plants of your area. Native plants will be adjusted to the growing conditions of your area. Thus, it will be able to adapt to the local climate and lighting changes. It will be easier for you to maintain such plants.

Almost all types of plants can be grown in container gardening. But, one thing that you will need to remember is that container gardening will not be altering the basic needs of the plants. Plants that are sun-loving will require lots of sunlight. The shade-loving plants will grow their best when kept under dappled light.

Drainage

No matter what type of plant you decide to grow in container gardening, drainage holes are very important. Without the presence of proper drainage, the soil in the container will tend to be waterlogged. It will eventually result in dying plants. The holes are not required to be very large but should be enough to allow the excess water to drain out of the container. In case containers come with no holes for drainage, you can drill some according to your need. Containers that come with no holes are used as a cachepot for hiding plain pots. Cachepots are very useful in managing heavy pots and large plants. You can grow plants in any ordinary pot that sits inside cachepot so that you can move the pots separately.

You can also opt for self-watering containers, hanging baskets, window boxes, and double-walled containers. These options can be helpful for dealing with plants that are of small size and need frequent watering. If you try to omit drainage in containers, you will be leaving the garden at high risk. Plants need water, light, and air to deal with their life in containers. Plant roots require water to deal with chemical processes of all kinds. It is also needed for transporting nutrients to the plants from the soil. Roots need air as well. In case the root systems of plants are left with no oxygen for a long period, the roots will suffocate. Thus, resulting in dead plants. Also, when you have excessive water near the root area, it can easily inhibit the availability of air.

Things turn out to be more complicated when you grow plants in containers. So, you will need to look after the drainage for ensuring adequate escaping of extra water. Proper drainage can help in improving the container soil structure, increases the effectiveness of phosphorus-based fertilizers, and conserves nitrogen. It also helps in preventing leaching and waterlogging.

Also, excessive drainage is not suitable for plants. In case you are experiencing excessive water drainage from the containers, you will need to water the plants more frequently. In case you fail to water the plants quickly, plants will dry out and will die. The main reason behind the problem of this kind could be container soil. It can happen if the soil is having an extreme proportion of sandy soil. Sandy soil cannot retain water effectively. On the contrary, if the soil is clayey, it might result in water stagnation. In such a case, it might result in root rot. The best solution for the problem of this kind is to add compost to the container soil before growing plants.

You can also opt for improving the soil structure to deal with drainage problems. You can add gravel or sand to improve the structure. You can also add rocks at the base of containers. This can be done with containers with holes and the ones that do not come with holes of any kind. In this case, the rocks at the base act like a reservoir, storing all the excess amount of water until the same get drawn up by the roots. For the containers with holes, the rock bed allows flowing out of excess water while preventing the soil particles and dirt from escaping. You can use gravels made from pebbles or granite. This is a very popular technique that is being used for container gardening by most gardeners.

Water

It is actually a tough job to determine the amount of water that is needed by container plants. A very fine line exists between soggy soil and drought soil, and either of the two can be dangerous for plant health. Summer is considered the toughest time for watering container plants. You can use a moisture gauge for easing your job of watering plants. Container plants have the tendency of drying out quickly when compared to the in-ground plants. The small amount of soil space, along with the container construction, can store a minimal amount of moisture. Generally, watering plants early in the morning or in the evening is considered the perfect time. This helps the plants to take in more amount of water before the day heat. It will also allow the plants to evaporate excess water. Thus the plants will not be vulnerable to any kind of fungus.

You will need to water the plants when the soil is dry, and that is a very common thing to do. But, only watering when the soil dries up might not be a good thing for the plants. Try to look out for limp stems, shriveled leaves, discolored leaves, and dropping petals. These are the signs of water deficiency. You will need to check the container plants daily in dry and warm conditions. Usually, when the top inch of the soil is dry, it is a good time to water the plants. You might need to water the plants twice in a day when the temperature goes above 85 degrees Fahrenheit.

If you are checking the containers all the time, you will know exactly when to water the plants. The frequency of watering will depend on the species and type of plant that you are growing. The drought-tolerant and succulent plants will need to be watered much less when compared to the annuals. The well-established plants can thrive longer without water than the plants that are newly installed. While watering the container plants, make sure that you water slowly so that the water can be accessed by every part of the root and soil. Light and short watering is most likely to get drained out of the holes much before the plants can actually take in some of the moisture. In fact, the majority of the container soil will start repelling water if left dried out for a long period. As you water deep and slow, it will ensure that the water reaches the roots of the plants. It will also force the dried soil to start absorbing water again.

In case the container soil has been completely dried out, it will be wise of you to soak the containers completely in a tub full of water. Soak the container for about 30 minutes or so for forcing rehydration of the soil. The amount of water that you will need to provide to the plants will vary greatly from one plant to the other. You can determine the average requirement of moisture of any specific plant and then get into use a moisture gauge. You will need to stick the gauge probe in the soil that will give you a reading about the level of moisture in the soil. If the container plants need moderately wet soil and the gauge shows readings in dry zones, you will need to water the plants. You can use glazed containers for preventing evaporation of water from the walls.

Tip: Water the plants when the temperature is cooler.

Logistics

Container gardening can be done anywhere without any kind of restriction. The best aspect of container gardening is that you can move the containers anywhere and anytime you want. It would be great if you can set up container gardening in the balcony, terrace, stairways, or even in your yard at a corner. Make sure that you do not keep containers on the sidewalk or near the entry gate. You can arrange the containers in benches by a corner to make the best out of the space you have.

While planning out the garden, make sure that you do not place the containers in spots that are prone to pests. You can move the containers anytime you want. Still, it is always better to prevent the onset of pests for avoiding future hassle. You can use hanging baskets for making use of the windowsill. The front yard can also be used, and in that case, you can place the containers close to a watering source.

Size

Growing your own vegetables in containers is a very popular and easy way of experiencing the flavors along with the freshness of homegrown crops. Here's a very well-known secret: most types of vegetables can grow very well in pots and containers. By choosing the perfect plants, you can easily create a small container vegetable garden and grow a decent amount of food within a few containers only.

But why give in the extra effort of growing veggies in containers rather than buying them from the market? Well, with the help of a container vegetable garden, you will be able to grow vegetables that you might not find in the market. Growing vegetables in containers is much easier than you think. Let's have a look at the perfect types and sizes of containers suited for your vegetable garden.

Types of Containers

Not sure what type of container to opt for your vegetable garden? It is not a problem at all as vegetables are not that fussy about the type of containers that they are grown in. The one and the only requirement for containers of a vegetable garden is that they need to be large enough for holding the plants. It should also have holes from drainage so that the extra amount of water can easily escape. Vegetables that are grown in clay containers are needed to be taken extra care of when compared to plants of other types. This is mainly because clay containers are porous in nature and can give out a lot of water via evaporation. You will need to pay attention to the color of the container as well. Do not opt for containers that are made out of treated wood as the chemicals can disturb the growth of the plants.

While talking about the size of the garden, there is no limit as such. The size of a container vegetable garden will depend solely on the size of the containers that are being used. But, keep one thing in mind, the bigger the container, the better will be the growth. This aspect works best for beginner gardeners. The main reason behind this is that large containers can hold more amount of soil. So, it can retain moisture for a longer period. So, you will not need to water the plants frequently. You can opt for vegetable growing containers that are 10 inches in width and 12 inches in depth. This is the ideal container size for beginners. Large-sized flower pots, window boxes, and large-sized containers of about 5 gallons will also work fine.

Certain vegetables need large pots for growing properly in a container garden. Tomatoes of standard size and vining veggies like cucumber can be grown the best in containers that are of 25 inches or even more across. Peppers can be grown, preferably in pots that are minimum 15 inches in diameter. However, vegetables of all size can be grown in containers of large size. Plants such as cucumber and tomato have the tendency to grow tall. They will produce vines that will be grown the best when provided with support in container gardening. You can use a wire cage that needs to be installed at the time of planting can provide the required support. You will need to use large and heavy containers for the trellised nature of plants. This needs to be done to minimize the overall risk of tipping.

Building Structures and Designs

In container gardening, everything is done in containers. So, there is no need for building any extra structure as the concept of container gardening moves around the easy movement of containers and plants. As there are is nothing like building structures in container gardening, we will be discussing the various types of container garden designs in this section.

Similar to decorating your home, a good decoration of containers is also a matter of self aesthetics. There will be several combinations of colors that will be appealing, while others will not. The secret to a great container design is to find out what your choice is and what you love. However, good designing of container gardening goes much beyond the choice of colors. It is more about partnering textures and pairing veggies and herbs in a pleasing manner. It is all about combining the perfect veggies with the perfect containers.

Proportion

Plantings that are not in proper proportion with the containers will tend to look top-heavy, flat, too dense, or not at all appealing depending on the design of the gardener. Design is important even if your goal is to set up a natural looking container garden and nothing that looks planned. You can start by looking at the container height. For proper proportion, the container that you have chosen needs to comprise of either 1/2 or 2/3 of the overall height of the container and plants combined. In simple terms, you need to aim for a ratio of 2:1 or 1:2. You will not be able to establish proper proportions until the appropriate height of the plants is reached.

Focal Point

Another vital point for container gardening design is to have one focal point. Many times the largest type of plant tends to be the focal point naturally because of its size. But, you can base the focal point of your garden on bold structures of a leaf, jazzy color, and vertical element. Try to keep only one focal point for each of the containers in the garden.

Designing With the Help of Edible Plants

Veggies and fruits are often cultivated in a utilitarian manner. Minimal thought is given to the layout and design of the container. There are various gardeners who love to focus on the productivity of the garden and not the layout and design of the container. But, you can actually do both great looking and highly productive garden in containers. The vessels containing vegetables can also be turned into something beautiful. There is no need for plunking the tomato plants in one large container all for themselves. You can grow tomatoes in the middle of a large container. It can be surrounded by herbs and short vegetable plants like peppers. You can also opt for spinach and lettuce for filling up the soil bed by the sides. Another great combination is to grow root crops like beets and carrots in the middle with sweet potatoes or cherry tomatoes by the sides. The design is all up to you. Just focus on not making the containers look clumsy.

Plants

Container gardening is a very effective way of saving space and growing fresh vegetables in any corner of your house. As you grow veggies in containers, you can easily deal with diseases and pests. Also, it takes much less time for growing plants than the conventional type of garden. You can also group plants that can help each other in containers. This technique is called companion planting. It will be easier for you to maintain the quality of plants as the allocated space is quite small.

Plant Journal

A plant journal can be maintained for keeping track of the plants that you have grown. It can help you maintain a record of the needs of the plants. Always keep in mind that you will need to mention the time of harvesting so that you can omit that plant for one or two years for effective crop rotation. It will be discussed in the later sections.

Spacing

You will need to provide the vegetable plants appropriate space for maturing. When you provide proper spacing to the plants, the roots of the plants will not need to compete with each other for moisture and nutrients. Also, proper spacing can ensure the right exposure of light to the plant surface that is required for growth. It also helps in proper air circulation. You can grow root and leafy vegetables in the containers with the use of seeds.

But, once they grow in size, you will need to thin them. Crops that provide fruits like peppers and tomatoes can provide the best produce when started in small pots of 3 – 4 inches and alter transplanted to large containers.

As you provide proper spacing to the plants, it will be easier for you to apply fertilizer to the plants. Also, the spreading of pests can be minimized.

Plants Suitable for Container Gardening

Various types of vegetables can be grown in containers. Let's have a look at them.

Beans

Green beans can be grown in containers and can act as a great addition to your courtyard or balcony. There are two proper ways of growing beans using containers. You can opt for the bush variety of beans that can grow very happily in containers without the need for any kind of support. The second one is the climbing variety and needs trellis for support. You can opt for the second option for making the best use of the vertical space as it is possible to run them on the fences and walls. Beans of any type need a minimum depth of 12 inches.

Beets

Beets are a great option for growing in confined spaces. The only aspect that you will need to focus on is to provide them with deep containers for proper development of the roots. You can pick a container of 12 -14 inches in depth for growing beet. You can grow various types of beets in containers such as Chioggia. This variety of beet comes with candy stripes with alternating white and red rings.

Chard

If a competition is conducted for finding the best-suited vegetables to be grown in containers, nothing can beat lettuces and leafy vegetables. Productive and fast-growing, this undisputed king of the world of edible plants makes a great choice as a potted crop. Lettuces and leafy green vegetables hardly need any space for thriving and come with a shallow root system.

Peppers

They are perfect for making the best use of small garden space. All that they need is a warm and sunny place for growing. You will need to provide them with a minimum container depth of 10 inches.

Companion Planting

There are various plants that can be grown together to help each other.

Salad Mix

You can grow a mix of salad vegetables that will be helpful for your cooking and also beneficial for the related plants. In a container of large size, you can grow tomato about 4 inches from the back of the container. As the plants mature, it won't shade the small plants. You can grow a combination of spinach and lettuce around the tomato plants. Sprinkle some seeds of carrots along the outer border of the container. Make sure that the arrangement you are going to make can provide room for the growth of individual plants. In case you want to aid the container from pests and insects, plant rosemary and sage by the sides.

Root Vegetables

Plant lettuce between various types of root crops like turnips, onions, beets, and carrots. It can help to retain the moisture of the soil and can also provide the soil with proper shade. Lettuce tends to grow very fast and can be harvested much before the growth of the root vegetables. So, plants in this type of combination can be grown close to each other for maximizing the available space. You can plant the root vegetables at the indicated distance on the pack of seeds and plant the seeds of lettuce in between. When any of the root crops mature, its foliage will provide shade to the soil when you start harvesting the lettuce.

Tomatoes

If you want to grow tomatoes in your garden, you can dedicate some of the containers for growing tomatoes along with their companions. In each of the tomato containers, plant chives or onions spaced narrowly in rows with the growth of carrots. You can grow cucumber with support along with tomatoes. You can also include few clumps of parsley along the corners of the containers. Marigold can be used as a border for repelling insects.

Squash and Beans

If you are willing to fill the garden with summer veggies, you can interplant beans with squash. Marigold can also be used for repelling insects. However, both beans and squash can grow in bush or vining form. You will need to grow either of the two in alteration of the other variety. For example, if you are growing beans of vining variety, you will need to grow squash of bush variety and vice versa. This way, either of the plants will be staying low and will shade the soil.

Crop Rotation

Crop rotation is all about moving vegetables all around the garden to maintain the fertility of the soil. In the case of container gardening, you can rotate crops among containers. As you rotate crops from one place to the other in the same season or the other, you will be able to preserve the nutrients of the soil. Some vegetables are heavy feeders like broccoli, tomatoes, cabbage, eggplant, corn, beets, and leafy vegetables. Light feeders include sweet potato, onions, garlic, peppers, radish, potato, and turnips. Soil builders include beans and peas. As you rotate these three groups of vegetables every season, you can make the best use of the soil nutrients.

Simple Rotation of Crops

This process includes planting heavy feeders in a container for the first year, followed by the group of light feeders the second year. The soil builders will be planted in the third year. This way, you will be able to preserve the quality of the soil and also grow vegetables of various types.

Rotating crops in containers might turn out to be a tough job if you have only a few containers. In such a case, you will still be able to opt for crop rotation. You can grow beans right after growing tomatoes. You can also replace a heavy feeding vegetable such as cabbage in the spring, peas in the fall, and beans in the next year.

Rotating Crops According to Harvest Groups

This is a very simple strategy for crop rotation. It includes rotating root crops, leafy crops, and fruiting crops. You can follow a simple crop rotation plan for three years divided into separate groups of harvesting.

- Leafy crops: Spinach, lettuce, and other members of the cabbage family like cauliflower, broccoli, and Brussels sprouts.
- Root crops: Potatoes, carrots, parsnips, and turnips.

- Fruiting crops: Peppers, tomatoes, cucumbers, eggplants, and squash.

In this mix, you can also add cover crops for following the fruiting crops. As most of the fruiting crops are grown during the summer – peppers, tomatoes, melons, squash, eggplants, they can be harvested during early autumn. So, the planting area of such crops can be used for replanting with winter cover crops like fava beans and winter rye. In the spring, the cover crop can be turned under, and you can grow leafy crops for continuing the crop rotation. The rotation will look like:

- Fruiting crop
- Cover crop
- Root crop
- Leafy crop

Crop Rotation With Plant Family

This is the traditional way of rotating crops, and it might be a bit tough for container gardening. In this method, crops that belong to the same family are not grown in the same container for over three to four years. It not only helps in maintaining the fertility of the soil but also acts as a great process for keeping away diseases and pests. If you tend to grow crops of the same family consecutively, pests and diseases will be more prone to them. Some of the notable plant families of vegetables that can be used for crop rotation in container gardening are:

- Squash family: Winter squash, cucumber, zucchini, melons

- Tomato family: Tomato, pepper, eggplant

- Cabbage family: Broccoli, cabbage, arugula, kale, collards

- Lettuce family: Artichokes, endive, sunchokes

- Bean family: Peas and beans

- Spinach family: Spinach, beet, sweet chard

- Onion family: Shallots, onion, leeks

- Carrot Family: Parsley, celery, parsnips, cilantro, fennel

Soil

Choosing soil for container gardening is not that difficult. But, the primary drawback that comes with container gardening is that the soil in the containers cannot be regenerated. They cannot gain extra nutrients from mother earth. The root system in container gardening cannot grow much deep into the soil. Plants that are grown in containers depend entirely on the growers for providing them with all that they need to survive. That is why you are required to choose the soil for container gardening properly. But how will you know which variety of soil will be the best for your garden? This section will be discussing various tips and suggestions for choosing the perfect soil for container gardening and which one to avoid.

Choosing Soil for Potting

Soil is regarded as the foundation for growing healthy plants. So, you will need to ensure that you use soil that is of high quality for growing plants in containers. When you start with a good mix of soil, you will be able to grow better quality plants. Good soil mix is expensive, indeed, but that is what will make all the difference. There are various types of soil that you will come across if you ever visit a local plant nursery. Soil also comes with a lot of dirt, and those are not at all suitable for growing plants in containers. Many beginner gardeners make the mistake of using soil from their garden or yard in the containers. You can grow plants using soil from the garden, but you will be actually taking a huge risk. First of all, soil from the garden is most likely to have nasty stuff like insects and bugs, weed seeds, disease organisms, etc. If you try using soil of this kind, you will be destroying your container garden with your own hands.

Secondly, garden soil is heavy in nature to be used for container gardening. It will tend to get compact very easily after a few days. In that case, plants will find it really difficult to grow in containers. So, it is always suggested not to opt for garden soil for containers and use only potting soil for ensuring the growth of the plants.

Best Soil for Gardening in Containers

It is important to choose soil of the best quality for container plants, but it is not required to be intimidating at all. If you are buying soil from outside, make sure that you check the label on it if it has been created for a certain purpose. For the majority of the outdoor plants, opting for an all-purpose mix of soil for container gardening is regarded as the best option. You can also choose soil by checking the consistency of the same. Here are some of the important things that you will need to look for a quality mix of soil.

- The soil is fluffy and light.

- The soil has good drainage. Make sure it can retain moisture that is needed.

- It is porous in nature so that air and water can reach the system of roots easily.

- There is no form of weed seed in the soil bag or any kind of tiny bugs.

- Make sure sand is not mixed with the soil.

- It needs to be moist in nature but not soggy. The smell needs to be pleasant.

Soil for Large Containers

Before opting for the type of soil that you will be using for container gardening, determine where you would like to place the plants. A mix of compost and soil will be heavier and is perfect for large containers. You will not need to think about the weight of the container as it will be sitting on the ground. So, you can opt for an all-purpose soil mix for large containers.

Soil for Hanging Baskets

When you decide to grow plants in hanging baskets, you will need to think about the container weight. You cannot make the basket too heavy with soil and water as it will be hanging. So, for hanging baskets, you can use a potting mix that is soilless. Soilless mixtures are made with coco coir or peat moss as the basic ingredient and are light in weight. Also, they do not come with sand or compost.

Reusing Container Soil

If you are trying to reuse container soil, you will be making a huge mistake. It might get contaminated with bugs and diseases from the last cultivation and can infect the new plants. Also, the soil will be having zero nutrients left as it will be used by the last grown plants. So, it will be better for you if you can dump used soil and start again with fresh soil. This way, you can ensure the proper growth of plants. But, if you have very deep containers, there is no need to replace the soil. You will need to remove above 4 – 5 inches of the topsoil and replace it with fresh soil before you start planting new crops. The soil amount that will be needed will depend on the size of the container that you will be using for growing plants. It can also vary according to the size and number of plants.

Before you fill soil in containers, make sure that the containers are clean. If you fill soil in dirty containers, it might result in an infestation of pests and diseases.

Planting

There are various vegetables that can grow the best in containers. Such vegetables include root vegetables, leafy vegetables, warm-season vegetables, and so on. In case you want to grow vegetables from transplants, you can do that. But, in container gardening, it is always suggested to grow vegetables from seeds.

Sowing Seeds

Many plants can start off better when grown in containers. You can even grow super fine seeds that cannot be grown using traditional methods. When containers are provided with adequate light and warm temperatures, the growth rate of plants can easily be improved. Make sure that you check all the information on the seed packet before sowing them in containers. You will get all the required information regarding watering and spacing on the seed packets. Before you sow the seeds, you will need to choose the type of container first in which you will be growing the plants. Cost, convenience, and reusability will be determining the type of container that you can use for sowing seeds. In case you are not able to water the garden daily, it will be better for you to opt for containers of 3 – 4 inches in diameter.

Plastic flats are the most widely used type of container that comes with no dividers at all. You can get them easily from any local gardening store. Sometimes you might even get them for free when you buy seeds. Next comes peat pots that are cheap but cannot be reused. The best aspect of the peat pot is that it minimizes the overall disturbance to the root system at the time of transplantation. But, you will need to keep them moist most of the time. You can also use plastic flats made from foam that has tapered cells. You can get them in various sizes, and some also come with capillary matting for drawing water from the soil. This can make the task of caring for the seedlings easier.

In addition to all the types of containers mentioned above, you can use items from your household as well, such as plastic cups, milk cartons, and so on. In case you are growing the seeds in this type of container, you will need to punch some holes at the base for ensuring proper drainage. You can sow the seeds directly in large containers, but make sure that you mark the spots if you are growing several types of plants at one time.

Process of Sowing Seeds

Materials Needed:

Soil Mix

Seeds

Container

Watering Can

Trowel

Procedure:

- You can start with your own soil mixture. You can also get soil mix from the garden stores that come with a combination of various essential elements. In case you want to make your own soil mix, mix peat moss, perlite, and vermiculite with soil from your garden.

- Dampen the soil mix before you fill-up the containers.

- Fill the containers up to the rim, leaving about ½ inch gap from the top. Firm the soil mix with your fingers.

- Check the information on the seed packet for the recommended depth of planting the seeds.

- You can either make furrows in the container with the help of trowel or simply scatter the seeds on the top of the soil.

- After you are done with scattering or sowing the seeds, you will need to cover the seeds with a fine layer of soil mix.

- If you are using individual pots for the individual types of seeds, you can label them. Mention the date of sowing to keep a record of the germination time.

- In case you are using small containers, you will have to cover the containers with damp newspaper. This will help in keeping the container soil moist for a long period while allowing air through it.

- Place the containers with sowed seeds in a warm spot for speedy germination.

- Ensure that you do not sow the seeds too deep; otherwise, the seeds will not be able to breathe.

Growing and Harvesting

Growing and harvesting in a container garden is not a tough job. But, there are certain aspects that you will need to take care of for ensuring the proper growth of plants.

Watering

Growing plants in containers come along with various benefits, but there are certain challenges as well. One of such challenges is correct watering. Proper watering is very important for the health of growing plants. While the majority of the people tend to get worried about under-watering of plants but in actual it is similarly easy to overwater the plants. As you over water the plants, you will bed drowning them. Make sure that the soil in the garden is moist and not soggy. However, different plants come with different requirements of moisture. There are certain plants that like to be dry, while some like to be a bit moist all the time. Juicy vegetables such as melons, cucumbers, and tomatoes like to be moist and thus needs a great amount of water. Herbs such as cilantro, basil, and thyme like to be in the middle, not too moist and not too dry. You will need to keep a regular tab on the requirements of your plants.

Before you water the plants, always check if the plants actually need watering. In most of the cases, the topsoil might feel dry, but it can be moist underneath. The easiest way of checking whether you need to water the plants is to stick your finger into the soil. If your fingertips feel dry, you will need to water the plants. If it feels moist, there is no need for watering the plants. The level of moisture can change very fast during hot and sunny days. So, a container that feels moist during the day might get dry by the afternoon.

When you water the plants, make sure that you give the plants a slow and long drink. Look for water coming out of the drainage holes at the base of the container. When you see water coming out of the holes, it means water has gone down to the base of the root tips which is required for the plants. Try to opt for shallow and frequent watering for making the roots of the plants to be at the top of the containers. This needs to be done in areas of drought and heat.

Plant roots tend to be more receptive to water during the morning and in the evening. So, whenever you decide to water the plants, make sure it is in the morning or in the evening. Out of the two options of watering the plants, watering during the morning is a better option. Watering during the evening will allow water to settle on the leaves, and this might result in fungal diseases like powdery mildew. Always note that you will need to water the soil and not the leaves. In case you water the leaves, the leaves might get sunburns. The droplets of water will act like small magnifying glasses and will burn the plant.

Even when you think that rainwater has watered the container plants properly, it is better to check the soil. Sometimes the foliage of plants and the flowers might act as umbrellas and can prevent the water from reaching the soil. In case you let the soil mix to get dry completely, it might stop absorbing water. If the soil gets dried out completely, poke holes on the soil surface, and give it a long and good drink. You might also need to water the plants more than once if the weather becomes too hot and dry. But, if you see wilting of plants during the day, do not opt for watering the plants immediately. Sometimes it might happen that the soil is moist and the plants still wilt. In such a case, the plants will get back to its normal state once the sun gets down.

Thinning

Growing vegetables using seeds is cheaper than using seedlings. But, it does involve some extra work. Many gardeners have the tendency to plant seeds of vegetables by sprinkling them in rows. As the seeds germinate, the seedlings are most likely to be spaced very close to one another. So, you will need to pluck the seedlings systematically for providing the other seedlings with the required room to grow. As you thin seedlings in container gardening, you will be able to produce healthy plants. You can have more yields simply by reducing the overall competition for getting nutrients and water from the soil. The plants will also be able to get better circulation of air.

You can thin the seedlings when they produce two to three leaves. Wait for the leaves to get about 3 inches tall for making the pulling task easier for you. In case you like to pull out the seedlings rather than cutting them with a scissor, thinning when the soil is moist and dry will make the whole task a lot easy for you. Every vegetable comes with its desired spacing.

- Carrots: 3 – 4 inches
- Beets: 3 – 5 inches
- Onions: 3 – 5 inches
- Lettuce: 15 – 18 inches
- Spinach: 3 – 6 inches
- Radishes: 3 – 4 inches
- Turnips: 3 – 4 inches
- Parsnips: 4 – 6 inches

Seedlings that are started from pots will not need thinning as you will be able to separate them at the time of transplanting. But, plants that you will be growing directly in the containers will need thinning. The number of seedlings that you thin or the spacing that you will be providing for the plants will rely on whether you want the vegetables to grow full size or you want them to harvest early. For instance, if you want tiny carrots, the seedlings can be spaced tightly. But, if you want large-sized carrots, you will need to provide the seedlings with more space.

Root vegetables might be very sensitive to the process of thinning, as disturbing the young root system can result in deformation.

Mulching

Mulching plays an important part in gardens of all types. You can add a layer of compost under the topsoil for retaining moisture. It can also help in deterring weeds. If the temperature of the soil tends to change drastically, it can be harmful to the plants. So, adding mulch to the soil can also help in regulating the soil temperature to a great extent. You can also use shredded leaves and straws for adding mulch to the soil.

Fertilizing

Just like watering, feeding the plants is also equally important. Plants that are grown using traditional methods in the soil can easily expand their roots for seeking nutrients. But, in the case of container gardening, plants cannot expand their roots outside the containers. So, it can be said that the plants grown in containers will be depending on your for their nourishment. You can use organic fertilizers for container gardening. But, the plants will be exhausting all the available nutrients within a few days. So, you can opt for liquid fertilizers for providing the plants with the required nutrients daily. You can make liquid fertilizer on your own or get some from the market.

You can find various types of liquid fertilizers in the market. You will need to check the N-P-K ratio on the pack. In this ratio, N stands for nitrogen, P stands for phosphorus, and K stands for potassium. You can get the fertilizer that comes with an equal proportion of all the three nutrients. For fruiting plants, you will need to get the fertilizer that comes with a higher value of K. If you are willing to make your own liquid fertilizer, you can get various information from the internet.

Fruiting veggies such as tomatoes will need to be fed weekly. But, make sure that you do not use fertilizer for the seedlings as it can burn out the plants. Generally, you can feed the plants in alternating weeks, maintaining the proportion suggested by the manufacturer.

Harvesting

You can harvest the vegetables either midway or after a full growing cycle. It is always better to harvest during the morning. If you are growing various types of veggies at the same time, you will need to keep track of their harvesting time. Different vegetables come with different periods of harvesting. However, it is better not to keep the vegetables for too long in the garden after the period of harvesting is over. It can result in pest infestation and diseases as well.

Weeding

Weed controlling in container gardening might turn out to be a daunting task. In the traditional gardens where weeding is possible by using sprays, it cannot be done in container gardening. The use of chemicals needs to be limited in container gardening. So, anything that you do regarding weeding needs to be done with your hands. You will need to keep the containers properly sanitized so that weeds cannot produce their seeds. After the harvesting period is over, and the containers are empty, try to chemically control the growth of weeds. You can install fresh stones or weed fabric if required. Herbicides can be used directly on the stones and weed fabric.

Pest Control

Controlling pests is a common problem that is shared by the majority of the gardeners of container gardens. The good aspect of container gardening is that container gardens are more accessible in nature and need frequent watering. You can find out problems before they tend to get out of your hands. Here are some steps that you can follow for effective pest control in container gardens.

- Do not try to reuse the potting mix. Try to avoid reusing the potting soil, specifically if it contained plants that were attacked by pests or diseases. Even when the soil looks okay, it might be contaminated with diseases and pests. Soil mix can also contain larvae or eggs of various insects.
- Try to clean the containers whenever you can. It can help in preventing pests to a great extent. Before planting new plants, scrub the containers with water and detergent. The containers that might have been subjected to diseases and pests need to be soaked in a bleach solution. Rinse the containers properly and permit them to get dried properly under the sun.

- Provide the plants with all that they need. You will need to provide the plants with the perfect combination of fertilizer, water, and sun. When the plants are healthy, they can easily fight against pests. Remove dead leaves and stems that can attract insects and pests.

- Do not try to keep infected plants in the garden. Some pests can spread very rapidly from one plant to the others. So, it is better to remove all those plants that are infected.

- Opt for regular inspection of the garden. If you notice something, take the necessary actions for dealing with the same before it spreads.

- Not all types of insects are harmful to plants. There are certain insects that can eat the harmful ones, for example, ladybugs.

Pros & Cons

There are various reasons that make container gardening a better option than traditional gardening. The primary benefit of container gardening is that you can move the containers wherever you want to. This section is all about the pros and cons of container gardening. Let's have a look at them.

Pros

- Containers improve the overall accessibility. It allows everyone to get indulged in gardening despite the various types of circumstances. You might have physical limitations that prevent you from bending down and gardening. With container gardening, problems of this kind can be solved. You can position the containers anywhere you want that can make working on them an easy job. Containers can make your dream of gardening turn into reality by providing you with the opportunity of decking up your balcony or terrace.

- Were you thinking about planting some vegetables for a long time but getting overwhelmed with the thought of managing them? In that case, container gardening can provide you with the required help. It is much more manageable because of the small size, and thus you can easily build your confidence in gardening. You can control the conditions of growing according to the needs of the plants.

- With the help of container gardening, you can get the chance of showcasing your creativity. Containers are available in shapes and sizes of all types. In fact, anything around you can be reused as a container for your garden when you use a little bit of your imagination, such as extra bathtub, watering cans, boots, and so on. You can create endless possibilities with container gardening with no form of restrictions at all. You can get the chance to decorate your windowsills as well.

Cons

- The containers tend to dry out faster. Although they can be placed anywhere, you will still need to water them frequently. The requirement of water increases during the summer heat when the soil in the container can dry out completely. You might even need to water them two to three times a day.

- You might need to provide the plants with additional feeding when compared to gardening in soil. This is mainly because the space in the containers is limited, and the system of roots cannot expand out for more nutrients from the soil. Even when you have the best medium of growth, supplemental feeding is necessary.

- You won't be able to use soil from the garden for filling the containers. So, you will need to buy soil mix from the market that is not cheap. The type of soil that you will need will depend on the type of plants that you are growing. So, if you are growing plants of various types at once, you will need to get the soil of different compositions.

- Plants can outgrow the containers. So, you will need to replace the small containers with large ones as the plants tend to grow bigger in size.

CHAPTER 3

In-Ground Gardening

There is something special about in-ground gardening that can easily announce to the world about your seriousness towards the pursuits of gardening. Maybe it is because this method has been nurtured for several years. Or, it is because the vegetables and fruits seem like they just sprung from Mother Nature. In-ground gardening is the most basic type of gardening that involves growing plants in your backyard or garden. It is simple in nature when compared to the other sectors of gardening and provides plenty of food when done right. It uses the soil that is available in the garden and thus can be regarded as an inexpensive way of growing crops on your own.

Well, as you decide to grow vegetables in your garden, you can enjoy several benefits. You will be able to make use of the area that is available to you without a problem of any kind. The best part is that there is no need to get soil from the outside if the soil in your garden is fine for growing plants. The majority of soils are perfect for gardening, provided that the soil is mulched, watered, and tilted. You can grow vegetables in your garden even without the use of any kind of amendments if the soil is fine for plant growth. You will be able to grow a plentiful harvest without any worries.

The work involved in starting up your garden is quite less. A flat area with proper drainage can be used for growing plants. You have the option of growing various types of crops at one time, without thinking about nutrients. This is because the root systems of plants can easily expand in the soil for getting extra water and nutrients. Also, the in-ground gardens tend to dry out less, and thus the requirement of water is also less. You can replace the garden with a crop of another type whenever you want.

You will not need to think about the shape of the garden, and you can make use of all the space that you have got. You can take advantage of the flat surface and will make the whole task of gardening a lot easier for you. However, if the soil in your garden is not that great, there is something that you can do. You will need to replace that with certain microbial agents that will help in regenerating the quality of the soil. If you want to grow large-scale crops at one time, in-ground gardening is the perfect choice for you. But, keeping away pests and diseases from the growing plants might turn out to be a challenge for you. As plants will be close to the ground, the infestation of pests will be more. You can add insecticides and pesticides to the plants, but it can degrade the soil quality to a great extent.

You can develop a checklist for all the required components such as water, sunlight, nutrients, and so on. It will make your task of gardening much easier. Let us start with the basics of in-gardening first, and then we will slowly progress to the other components of the same.

Basics

In-ground gardening will also need some of the basic components for growing plants such as water, nutrients, drainage, sunlight, and so on. For getting the most out of your garden, you will need to make sure that plants are getting all that they need in proper quantities.

Sun

The majority of the plants need about 6 – 8 hours of full sunlight per day. So, you will need to set up the garden in such a spot where sunlight is available readily all throughout the day. You will need to observe your garden to find out which place receives the best sunlight with no shade. In case your garden is under shade the majority of the time, there is nothing to worry about. You won't be able to grow vegetables like tomatoes in the shade, but the cultivation of other veggies and fruits is possible. Never try to omit the step of proper sunlight as plants won't be able to thrive without light. So, when you choose the spot, choose it wisely. You will need to arrange the plants in the way of making the best use of light and space. You can group the tall vegetables on the northern side of your garden. This will make sure that the tall plants won't shade the shorter ones.

It is always better to grow small and fast-maturing vegetables between the large plants. In case the temperature rises a lot, you will need to protect the plants from excess heat. Sunlight is necessary for plant growth, but an excess of it can dry out plants.

Drainage

The drainage system can actually create havoc for your vegetable garden, specifically after a period of heavy rain. When the drainage of your garden is poor, the logged water can prevent oxygen from reaching the roots and thus will result in dying plants. Also, when you have logged water near the root area, it can lead to root rot. It can give rise to fungus and pest infestation as well—the majority of the drainage problems of in-ground gardening results from clayey soil. Clay soil is denser than loamy or sandy soil. So, it allows the rainwater to filter out very slowly. Not only rainwater, but normal garden watering also needs proper drainage.

To prevent problems of drainage, make sure that the area of gardening is higher than the surrounding areas. In case the spot of gardening is lower than the surrounding area, water will get logged easily. You can also create an underground drain for an effective solution of drainage. The most widely used type of underground drain is the French drain. You will need to make a ditch all around the garden filled with gravel. You can create a small drainage system for redirecting water out of the garden bed. Maintaining drainage for in-ground gardens might turn out to be a tough job.

Water

Watering the plants will be of no value if the water tends to run down the area of the root system. This is most likely to happen when you water the plants quickly or supply too much water at a time. Watering is most effective when done slowly. When it comes to the watering of an in-ground garden, there is no definite rule. It will depend completely on the idea and knowledge of the gardener. It is a kind of judgment that will rely on various things such as soil, plant type, time, weather, and several other variables. As you build up a garden on your own, you will get an idea about the needs of the plants. You can get proper knowledge first about the various types of plants before planting them in your garden. This will help you to determine the water requirement for the plants.

No matter how much you water or how often you water, make sure that you do it in the morning. This helps in proper absorption of water by the plant roots while the excess water gets dried off by the day heat. Also, it can prevent the plants from various types of diseases and pests. For in-ground gardens, you can use an automatic timer for watering the plants along with a sprinkler. This can ease up your job a lot. You will just need to ensure the weather and adjust the frequency of watering according to that. During the hot summer days, you might even need to water the plants two to three times a day. You can also use mulch to prevent water runoffs. In case the plants need precise watering, you can opt for a drip system. It will help in providing the plants with the required amount of water.

In case the garden soil is heavy in nature, water might take a long time to get to the plant roots. So, make sure you water the plants slowly and allow the plants a long drink.

Tip: Try to use a shovel for checking the progress of water up to the root system.

Logistics

Make sure that you establish the garden in a place that is free from pests and diseases. While setting up the garden, you will need to leave some space all around the garden for proper accessibility from all sides. In case you are growing plants in rows, you can leave a wide space between the rows that will make the task of planting, weeding, watering, and others easier for you. Do not make the garden too constrained, otherwise it will be turn out to be tough for you to manage the garden.

If you want to set up a large garden, try to set it up close to the water source. Make sure that all the tools and equipment are handy in your garden. You will need to leave some space for transportation, for example, a wheelbarrow. Try to set up the garden away from large trees as it can shade the garden.

Size

In case you are confused about the size of your vegetable garden, there is no definite size for it. According to some gardeners, having a garden of 100 sq. Ft. is a perfect size, while for some, it is 150 sq. Ft. All these 'perfect' sizings cannot be correct as different families come with different needs. Also, the plants will vary in size. So, the size of the garden will depend on the type of vegetables that you want to grow.

You can find out the size of your garden by determining the purpose of your garden first. Do you want to set up the garden for your kitchen supplies, or do you want to depend on the garden for everything? This is the basic thing that you will need to determine. People set up their garden for various reasons; some want a garden for their hobby while some want to grow some large-size produce. Also, the number of heads that you are trying to feed will affect the garden size. Obviously, if you are the only person who will feed on the garden produce, the size of the garden is not required to be huge. If your family has four members, you will need a garden that is smaller than a family of six and vice versa. It might be a bit tough to assume all these in the first if you are only a beginner in gardening.

If you are opting for succession planting, the size of the garden can be small. For example, if you are willing to grow beans and peas in the same garden, peas can be grown in February, and beans can be grown after that. There are several other plant combinations that are good for the garden. It will be discussed in the upcoming sections. Many people opt for several garden beds at one time. In this, you will need to divide the total garden into several sub-parts. This has nothing to do with the garden size directly but is essential while planning the size of your garden.

The number of times that you will be planting in a year will also determine the size of the garden. You can grow a summer garden with squash, tomatoes, peppers, and cucumbers and then a winter garden with squash, cabbage, and other root vegetables. You can finish off with spring garden of spinach, lettuce, peas, and cabbage. This might seem like more tiring than having one or two gardens per year. But, when done properly, it can help in saving a lot of space. The types of vegetables that you are willing to grow also play an important role. You will need more space for growing tomatoes than carrots or any other root vegetable. Just keep one thing in mind; different plants need a different area for growing. It could actually make more sense to grow small plants with higher yields than growing large vegetables with poor yield.

Building Structures

In-ground does not any kind of structure as such. But, you can make certain structures for providing support to plants of various types. Plants such as peas, beans, and tomatoes might need support when they grow in size. In such cases, you can use a trellis or other supportive structures for the plants.

Before you opt for building a structure for plants, you will need to look after your purpose and budget as well. In case you are looking out for a very basic support system, designing a trellis with sticks and ropes will be fine. But, if you want to create a support system for many plants at one time, you will need a sturdier one. You can also build small fences around the garden to prevent pests and animals from damaging the garden. There are various designs of trellis that you can try out. One such popular design of trellis is the window frame. It is quite easy to build, and you will need a few basic things for building.

Materials Needed for Window Frame Trellis
Old door or window frame

Nails

Hammer

Tape measure

Galvanized wire

Process:

- Place the frame on a surface that is accessible from all sides.

- Start putting nails on the frame at a gap of 6 inches. Use a tape measure for measuring the gap.

- After you are done with putting the nails, now it is time to use the wire for making the mesh.

- Start by placing the wire vertically from one side to the other.

- Now, place the remaining wire horizontally from one side to the other. This way, you will be able to make a cubic wire network on which the plants can take support.

- You can now place the frame where you want to and start planting.

Plants

Growing your own vegetables is always rewarding and fun. But, as you start with it, you will need to begin with a few numbers of plants and good quality of the soil. For being a successful gardener, you will need to understand the requirement of the plants and plan accordingly.

Plant Journal

Keeping a plant journal is very important while growing plants in an in-ground garden. This is because as you will be growing plants over a vast area, it won't be possible for you to maintain them without proper records. It is beneficial when you will be growing plants of various types in your garden. You can maintain a separate journal for each area of the garden bed.

Spacing

The location where you will be setting up the garden is very important. Making the most out of your garden space is much crucial than growing vegetables. Most gardeners dream of having a huge garden of vegetables, a huge site that will be enough for growing anything they want. But, despite that, you will need to maintain the spacing of your garden properly. Whether you want to create a dense vegetable garden or a moderate one without proper spacing, plants cannot grow. This applies especially for in-ground gardens where several plants are grown at one time.

Maintain a space of about 5 – 6 inches between the plants. The best way of maximizing space in your garden is to get rid of rows. Row gardening is suitable for large-scale gardening, but for a home garden, the fewer rows you have, the less space you will need to leave between them. Thus, you will be able to utilize more square feet of the garden while leaving the required space in between.

Companion Planting

Companion planting is important for in-ground gardening. As you grow plants that are compatible with each other, you will be able to control weed, disease, and pests, improve soil quality, and so on. Companions help each other to grow properly and also use the space of the garden efficiently. For example, tall plants can help in providing shade to light-sensitive plants. Vines can help in covering the soil surface while stalks can grow tall.

Roses and Garlic

You can grow rose with garlic as the smell of rose can help in repelling garlic pests. Also, the chives of garlic help in repelling insects that attack rose plants.

Cabbage and Tomato

When you grow tomato and cabbage together, tomato helps in repelling larvae of diamondback moth that feeds on the leaves of cabbage. The moths tend to create large holes on the cabbage leaves that can be prevented by growing tomato plants side by side.

Dill and Cabbage

Cabbage and dill act as a great companion. Dill can be grown with the plants of the cabbage family, such as Brussels sprouts and broccoli. Cabbage helps in providing support to the floppy structure of dills. On the other hand, dills help by attracting useful wasps that can control worms and pests that attack cabbage.

Beans and Corns

Beans help in attracting important insects that can eat away pests of corn like leaf beetles, leafhoppers, and armyworms. The vines of beans can also seek the support of corn stalks.

Spinach and Radish

Planting spinach along with radish can keep away leafminers from the green leaves of radish. Leafminers can also eat away leaves of radish.

Crop Rotation

Crop rotation is an important aspect of in-ground gardening. As you tend to grow crops in the ground, fertility, along with nutrient content of the soil, can get low. Following the system of crop rotation for your garden is a proven way of improving the condition of the garden, without the use of external components.

The main idea behind the concept of crop rotation is to cultivate each group of plants in different parts of the garden every year. The goal is to improve the overall yield along with the health of the plants that you grow in your space. You will need to split the crops into various groups according to their habits and needs. Plants that are of the same type can grow better together. It will be easier for you to provide them with exactly what they need. Also, different crops take different types of nutrients from the soil and are most likely to leave behind certain traces. If you tend to grow the same types of plants every year in the same place, it will be deteriorating the structure and fertility of the soil steadily.

Crop rotation is very effective in dealing with issues of this kind. One of the most basic systems for rotating the crops is by splitting them into four different groups and then plant them in a rotation schedule of four cycles.

Plant Groups for Crop Rotation

The large-scale growers can develop various types of complicated systems that involve green manures, fallow years, and several other considerations that are industry-specific. But, if you are trying to opt for a small home-grown garden and willing to rotate the crops, you can split them into four simple groups.

- Brassicas: This group consists of kale, cabbage, Brussels sprouts, broccoli, cauliflower, kale, and other friends of this group. This group of crops is prone to clubroot disease that tends to build up in the soil very quickly when the same crops are grown repeatedly in the same soil.

- Legumes: Beans and peas are the most common members of this group. This group of crops helps in fixing nitrogen in the soil. Thus, they can work as a natural fertilizer for all the crops that follow them in the system of crop rotation.

- Potatoes: Although potatoes are an underground crop, they are treated as a group of rotation within their own growth. The primary reason behind this is that the harvesting process of potatoes needs excessive digging of the soil. This acts as an important role in the rotation. You can also grow chilies, tomatoes, and peppers within this group as they come with the same kind of requirement.

- Roots: This group consists of several plant families. But, each member crop produces an important portion of the crop under the soil. Some of the most common examples are onion, garlic, carrot, beets, and radish.

Crop Rotation and Its Benefits for In-Ground Gardening

Apart from the benefits of crop rotation that you have already learned from the previous chapters, crop rotation comes with other benefits as well.

- As you grow crops of the same group together, they will have similar harvesting and sowing times. So, it will make the process of space management much easier.

- Different groups of plants come with different root system depth. Crop rotation helps in spreading the nutritional load over several layers of the soil year after year. This will provide the layers more time for recovery.

- Similar group of crops can benefit from common mulching, watering, and also feeding regimens.

- Crop rotation also helps in preventing pests that are crop-specific from establishing in the garden.

Planning Crop Rotation

Before you star crop rotation in your garden, it will be better for you to make a working plan first. Start by dividing the garden into four different sections. Make sure that each section has adequate drainage, sunlight, and also protection from wind. You will need to set aside each plot for each of the plant groups for every year of the crop rotating cycle. After that, you will need to move each section of the crop down the other section by following this list.

- Group 1: Legumes

- Group 2: Brassicas

- Group 3: Onions and roots

- Group 4: Potatoes

It is very important to plant the crops in this order. It works the best as in the very first stage, legumes will take nitrogen from the air and will fix the same in the soil. Brassicas will be able to thrive on the extra nitrogen and is the best for following legumes in the rotation cycle. As you plant roots after brassicas, nutrients from the lower part of the soil will be used up while providing the upper level of the soil a chance for recovery. In the last, as you dig up the soil, the soil will get a thorough rejuvenation at the end of the rotation cycle.

You can follow another rotating crop cycle in which the steps are identical, like the previous one.

- Group 1: Legumes – Beans and peas

- Group 2: Leaf crops – Cabbage, spinach, rocket, lettuce, etc.

- Group 3: Root crops – Turnip, onion, radish, carrot, potato, etc.

- Group 4: Fruit crops – Pumpkin, tomato, cucumber, eggplant, capsicum, zucchini, etc.

It is true that crop rotation is not meant for everyone. You will need proper knowledge along with planning for carrying out successful crop rotation. But, if you are willing to use natural and sustainable methods most of the time, crop rotation can act as an effective and essential technique for use.

Soil

Healthy soil can guarantee you with healthy plants and also a healthy garden. When you keep the garden soil in proper shape, you will not need pesticides and fertilizers for the soil. Organic soil comes with a high proportion of humus. Humus is the final result of decaying objects such as grass clippings, leaves, and compost. It can hold water very well but also comes with great drainage qualities. Good garden soil will be fluffy and loose in character. It needs to be filled with air that is needed for the plant roots. It also needs to have enough minerals to assist in the proper growth of plants.

Soil pH

The pH of the soil needs to be neutral for ensuring the proper growth of plants. Having a pH level between 6.0 and 6.8 is taken to be the best. There are certain plants that need acidic soil for growing. But, such plants cannot be included within the group of garden vegetables. Wood ash can be used to raise the level of pH. But, make sure that you do not use an excessive amount of wood ash as it can result in increasing the level of pH excessively. It might also take away nutrients from the soil. So, proper care needs to be taken. You will need to spread a light amount of the same on the topsoil during fall. Ensure that you turn the soil properly during the spring.

Soil Density

Along with the pH of your garden soil, it is also very important to determine the texture and density of the same. The texture and density of the soil will depend on the total amount of silt, sand, and clay that it holds. Sand is composed of the biggest particles of soil and feels gritty when touched. Silt particles tend to be slippery when moist and feel like powder as you dry them. You are not required to be an expert in determining the density and texture of the soil. All that you need to do is to take a small amount of soil in your hand and rub it with your fingers. The soil is sandy in nature if it feels gritty. If it feels powdery, the soil is silty. If the soil tends to feel sticky when moist and harsh when you dry it, the soil is clayey in nature.

The majority of the soil will be somewhere in between. You will need to have a kind of soil that drains well and is not sticky in nature. If the soil is rich in clay, it might turn out to be a problem for drainage and might result in waterlogging.

Mix

As you add compost to the soil, it can improve the soil quality. You can get some organic compost from the market and mix it in the soil before planting the crops. Compost, along with other types of organic matter, helps in holding the soil particles together and retains moisture very well. The soil will be able to reserve the nutrients as well that are made available for the plants. Make sure that you mix the garden soil from the bottom for mixing all the components of the soil properly. If you just try to dig in the topsoil and start planting crops, it will result in poor growth of plants.

You can use mulch like straws, leaves, shredded bark, and so on for covering the soil. It will help in protecting the soil from high heat and also cold. It will also help in dealing with water loss. Mulching is also effective in deterring the growth of weeds.

Maintenance

Maintaining the nutrients and pH of the soil is not enough for the proper growth of plants. You will need to remove debris from the soil so that pests and diseases cannot develop. One of the primary things that you will need to check is the soil after a period of heavy rain. You can also get a pH meter for keeping a check on the level of pH. Make sure that you opt for removing weeds from the garden soil. If not done properly, weeds can easily destroy the entire garden.

Planting

Spacing in in-gardening matters the most as you have less control over the quality of the soil. The space that you will need to maintain will depend on the types of plants that you will be growing. In case you are growing vining types of vegetables in the garden, you will need to prepare trellis or other support systems for the plants as you sow the seeds.

For growing vegetables in the garden, you can sow the seeds directly in the soil without opting for transplants or seedlings. Well, if you want, you can also grow veggies from transplants. But, in most cases, direct sowing of seeds is preferred.

There are various plants that can grow the best when the seeds are sowed directly in the soil. But how to do that? Well, there are two methods that you can use for sowing the seeds directly in the soil: hill method and trough method. The method that you will choose will rely on the seed type that you are sowing. In case you are not sure which method to opt for, check the description on the seed packets.

Hill Method

In this method, you will need to pile the soil into a mound. This will help in heating up the soil quickly. This is beneficial for the small seeds as they need warmth for germinating. You will need to pile the garden soil into a mound that is about 1 – 2 feet in diameter and about 5 inches in height. Use your fingers for poking small holes at a distance of one to two inches apart in the mound top. You will need to plant one seed in each hole. In case you are not sure about the depth of sowing the seeds, check the seed packet.

After you are done with sowing the seeds, water the seeds gently, you will need to thin the seedlings after they germinate.

Trough Method

This is the simplest way of planting seeds in your garden. You will need to use two fingers for digging a shallow trench. Sprinkle the vegetable seeds evenly and lightly along the trench. Apply a thin layer of soil from the top for closing the seed trench that you have dug. Ensure that you check the details on the seed packet for the depth of sowing the seeds. Moisten the topsoil of the trench gently.

In this case, also, you will need to thin the seedlings as they germinate. In case you are unsure about the spacing of the seedlings, you can check the details on the seed packet.

You can directly sow seeds of root vegetables. They cannot be transplanted well as seedlings as it can disturb the root system. Crops that love heat such as pepper, eggplant, and tomato need long seasons for producing. They cannot grow well when sown directly in the soil. It is better to start them as seedlings from indoors and then transplant the same in garden soil. Other heat-loving crops like squash, cucumber, and pumpkin can be sown directly.

Growing and Harvesting

The growing and harvesting of vegetables that are grown in home gardens can be done very easily. You will need to follow certain tips and suggestions for getting the best results.

Watering

For preventing the growing plants from wilting in hot weather, you will need to water the plants properly. But, how often and how much you will need to water? Majority of the plants depend on proper moisture levels. So, even slight drying of the soil and plants can disturb the plant growth.

Watering Less and Thoroughly

You can water the plants three to four times a week when the temperature is moderate. But, when it is extremely hot, you might even need water the plants two to three times every day. But, it is always better to water the plants with plenty of waterless often rather than watering less often. You will need to ensure that the plants you water during the morning or evening only. As you water cool soil in the morning or in the evening, less amount of water will evaporate when compared to watering during the heat of the day.

Keep the Leaves Dry

It is very important to keep the plant leaves absolutely dry. When you water the leaves, it might give rise to diseases. Also, when you water the leaves in the sun, it can result in burn marks. If leaves are left wet overnight, it can attract fungus and pests.

Avoid Waterlogging

Make sure that water does not get logged near the root area as it can make it difficult for the plant roots to breathe properly.

Thinning

Thinning of plants is a necessary practice that needs to be done for allowing the plants with proper room for growing. Thinning provides the plants with all the requirements for proper growth, such as light, moisture, nutrients, and so on. As you thin seedlings, you will also be able to improve the circulation of air near the root area of the plants. It is important to understand the proper time for thinning the seedlings. In case you are late, overdeveloped roots can damage the other seedlings during the process of thinning. Relying on the type of plants that you are growing, you will need to thin the seedlings enough so that each seedling can have two to three inches of space on all sides.

Learning the process of thinning is not that tough. But, not all plants will be able to handle the process of thinning in the same way. For example, plants that come with a fragile system of roots like cucurbits and beans need to be thinned as fast as possible, before the roots get intertwined with each other. The main aim is to pull out the seedlings that you do not want in the garden, leaving back the healthy seedlings. Root crops are slightly sensitive to the process of thinning and needs to be done with extra care.

Mulching

No matter what you grow, you will need to provide mulch to the soil. It can help in improving the drainage system and also helps in dealing with weeds. It is always recommended to mulch in layers.

Fertilizing

The main key to proper fertilizing is timing. You will need to provide fertilizer to the plants and soil, depending on the needs of the same. Fragile young plants such as tomatoes and pepper might it difficult to deal with fertilizer if applied at an early stage. It can burn the root system of the tender plants. Also, as you decide to use fertilizer for the plants, you will need to determine the needs of the plants. Fertilizers come in various compositions of nutrients, and each plant comes with separate requirements of nutrients.

Harvesting

For getting the best taste of the vegetables from the home garden, you will need to harvest at the perfect time. There is no fixed rule for harvesting. For the best texture and flavor, most of the veggies are harvested before their full maturity. Here are some examples of harvesting vegetables.

- Beans: The perfect time for harvesting beans is before the seeds start bulging. You will need to check them regularly as beans take very little time in going from tough to tender.

- Carrots: It is quite tough to find out the perfect time for harvesting carrots. The top part of the carrot can be seen at the line of soil, and the diameter for your preferred variety can also be seen. In the majority of the cases, if the diameter looks fine, the length will be perfect too.

- Corn: Right after 3 – 4 weeks after the formation of the silk, they will start turning brown and dry. This is the time when you will need to check the kernels. If the kernel gives out milk-like substance when pricked with nails, it is time to harvest.

- Lettuce head: You can harvest lettuce heads when the heads feel firm and full. Very hot weather might result in the bolting of the heads.

- Onion: You can harvest onion right after the top part falls over. You will need to dry the onion before storing it.

- Peas: The pea pods need to feel and look full. You can enjoy sweet peas if you can harvest them before getting plump. You can taste peas before harvesting them.

Weeding

Weeding is very important in gardens of all types. You can opt for weeding during the early morning as the dew can help in turning the soil loose. For deterring weeds for a long time, you can turn the soil regularly. If weeds develop, do not waste any time and pull them out as soon as possible. Mulching can help in minimizing the growth of weed. Remove dead stems and leaves from the garden. Do not keep the garden soil too moist as it can promote the growth of weed. Weeds can eat up soil nutrients, and so proper care needs to be taken.

Pest Control

The majority of gardeners face the problem of pest in their vegetable garden, especially before the time of harvesting. But, sometimes, the infestation of pests can rise to an excessive level. The small-sized pests can create a lot more disturbance in the garden than you can actually think of. Till now, the most useful way in which pests can be controlled is by preventing them from entering the garden. Prevention of pests is not that tough if done properly.

- **Encouraging useful insects:** Beneficial insects can help in eating the small pests that mulch on the growing crops. Lacewings, ladybugs, damsel bugs, pirate bugs, and parasitic wasps are some of the beneficial insects. They can help in keeping the number of pests under proper control. For attracting insects of this kind, you will need to supply them with nectar-rich in carbohydrates. The more beneficial insects you can have in the garden, the more you can keep the infestation of pests under control.

- **Choosing garden plants wisely:** There are certain varieties of plants that are more prone to get infested by pests than others. Prevention of pests in the garden is sometimes as easy as opting for the pest-resistant crops. For instance, if squash bugs tend to attack plants of winter squash, royal acorn can be used as the resistant variety.

- **Employing physical barriers:** A very useful way of preventing pests is by using physical barriers in the garden that can keep out pests from the plants. You can cover the plants that are susceptible to pests with the use of row cover. Make sure that you tuck in the sides of the cover properly for preventing the sneaky pests from getting inside. But, keep in mind that you will need to open the covers when the plants are ready to flower or produce fruits.

- **Intercropping:** You can prevent pests in the garden by improving the diversity of vegetable growth in your garden. As you start inter-planting various vegetable plants with one another and also with flowering herbs, it will become difficult for the pests to locate the host plants. So, instead of just planting one type of crop in the garden, try to grow two to three varieties of vegetables at once. There are pest-repellent varieties as well that you can learn from the companion planting guide in the next chapter. When you inter-plant, the pests will find it difficult to hone on their dinner.

Pros & Cons

In-ground gardens come with a wide array of pros and cons. It provides several benefits over the other sectors of gardening, such as container gardening and others. Let us have a look at them.

Pros

- You can have more control over the quality of the garden soil. You can easily adjust the texture, condition, and quality of the soil that is suitable for growing crops. Soil composition can be adjusted by adding in certain elements that you need for improving the quality of the soil. You can add organic matter for adding texture and nutrients to the soil.

- The plants can establish deep root systems. As the root system becomes large, the plants will turn out to be bigger and tasty. Also, plants can get the required amount of water and nutrients from the soil by extending the system of roots. So, plants will be able to thrive better in in-ground gardens. The moisture retention power of the soil will also be better, and thus the plants will not suffer from lack of water.

- This form of gardening makes the task of applying fertilizer and insecticides a lot easier. You can spray them wherever you need to.

- You can opt for better drainage by digging a trench all around the garden. You can also use artificial drainage systems to ensure proper drainage.

- You can have more control while controlling pests.

- The cost of setting up an in-ground garden is not that much. There is no need for any extra material, which is the case in raised bed gardening. You will be growing plants from the garden soil only. There is no need to get expensive soil from the market. No extra setup other than trellis and support systems is required as the crops are grown without the use of structured frames.

Cons

- This form of gardening needs more skills and knowledge for growing plants. As the area of growing plants is most likely to be larger than the other sectors of gardening, you will need to be more cautious about the growth of the plants.

- In case you opt for transplantation of the crops, the shock of transplantation can delay the time of harvesting.

- You will need to give more attention while watering the plants. This is because, in this sector of gardening, the majority of water can drain off if the water is supplied at high speed.

- As you will be sowing seeds directly in the garden, you will need to give in more time for thinning the seedlings. Also, thinning might turn out to be a tough job as the seeds will be sown directly in the soil.

- It might turn out to be tough for you to start growing the direct-sown vegetables in hot and cold conditions.

- The plants will take more space if sown directly without the use of transplants. Also, space management might turn out to be a tough thing.

CHAPTER 4

Plant Profiles

Plant profiles can help you in making your gardening venture a lot easier. This chapter is all about the plant profile of various garden plants.

Basil

Scientific name: Ocimumbasilicum

Details: Basil can be grown in the garden for creating wraps. Purple-colored basil can help in creating a focal point in the garden.

Family: Lamiaceae

Season Of Growing: Spring and late spring

Zone: Three through ten

Spacing: Twelve to eighteen inches

Seed harvesting: 40 – 90 days

Seed starting (indoor): 7 – 8 weeks before frost

Outdoor planting (earliest): After frost danger. Ground temperature needs to be 65 degrees Fahrenheit.

Watering: One-inch water every week during the cycle of growth.

Starting

Location: Needs to be full sun

Planting: You will need to cover the seeds with one-inch soil if you plant the seeds directly in your garden.

Growing

You cannot allow basil to dry out. Watering daily is the best thing. For creating bushy plants, you will need to pinch off the top parts of the plants as they start flowering.

Harvesting: You can pull off the basil leaves whenever desired.

Problems: In case you have opted for growing basil in a very warm spot, you will need to choose those varieties in which bolting takes place slowly.

Bell Pepper

Scientific name: Capsicum annum

Details: Bell pepper can be used as a crop for rotation. Do not opt for growing bell peppers in the same place where you have grown peppers, tomatoes, or eggplant the previous year.

Family: Solanaceae

Season of growing: It is best suited for warm climates such as early spring or late spring before summer days. It can also be grown in slightly cold climates.

Zone: Three through ten

Spacing: Fifteen to seventeen inches apart

Seed harvesting: Sixty-five to seventy-five days

Seed starting (indoor): Ten weeks before the last frost. In extreme southern regions, you can plant the seeds in the garden soil directly.

Outdoor planting (earliest): During early spring right after the last frost.

Watering: Two to three inches of water every week.

Starting

Location: Conditions of full sun is needed

Planting: Cover the seeds with a thin layer of soil after sowing.

Growing

If excessive nitrogen is provided to the plants, more leaves will be produced than peppers.

Harvesting: It is better to cut the peppers from the stem instead of just pulling the peppers off. Peppers tend to develop more flavors with time.

Problems: Bell peppers are very much prone to aphids. You can use water and natural soap to deal with them. You might also face the problem of blossom end rot. This type of condition typically gets cleared on its own. In such a case, you can cut out the portion that is affected and consume the fresh part. Another problem that comes with bell pepper is the cucumber mosaic virus. You will need to spend some extra time in pulling out the infected plants and then dispose of the same. In case you face the problem of cucumber mosaic virus, try to opt for a different spot for growing the next year.

Cabbage

Scientific name: Brassica oleracea var. capitata

Details: Some types of cabbage can grow flowers. The leaves of cabbage can be eaten. But, in the majority of the cases, the leaves are used for the purpose of garnishing. You can check the packet of seeds for verifying if the leaves are edible.

Family: Brassicaceae

Season of growing: Plant the seeds during early spring or during late fall

Zone: Three through ten

Spacing: Twelve to seventeen inches apart

Seed harvesting: Fifty to sixty days

Seed starting (indoor): Six to sex weeks before the onset of the last frost

Outdoor planting (earliest): During early spring after you can work on the garden

Watering: You will need to keep the plants properly watered during dry conditions

Starting

Location: Conditions of full sun is needed

Planting: Cabbage plants can easily withstand very light frost

Growing

Cabbage plants come with a very shallow system of roots. You will need to take proper care while cultivating or weeding so that you do not damage the root system.

Harvesting: You can harvest cabbage when the top heads feel firm.

Problems: One of the primary problems of cabbage plants is cabbage aphids. You will need to use strong water spray or insecticidal soap for removing them. Cabbage worms are also very common. You can remove them with your hands or use row covers for keeping them away. In the case of clubroot, you will need to remove the infected plant. If cutworms attack the cabbage plants, you can remove them with your hands.

Broccoli

Scientific name: Brassica oleracea var. italic

Details: If you are willing to grow broccoli in a warm climate, opting for the fall planting will be the best for you. This is because broccoli can easily survive in cold weather.

Family: Brassicaceae

Season of growing: You can grow broccoli during fall, spring, and cool weather.

Zone: Three through ten. In case you live in a warmer zone, you will need to use seeds that are tolerant to heat.

Spacing: Eighteen to twenty-five inches in each row at a distance of three feet apart

Seed harvesting: Fifty to sixty days

Seed starting (indoor): Seven to eight weeks before the period of the last frost of spring. You will need to provide the seedlings with light of fifteen to seventeen hours with the help of fluorescent lighting.

Outdoor planting (earliest): You can plant them before two weeks of the last frost of spring. During fall or warm climates, you can do it ninety to a hundred days prior to the first frost.

Watering: You will need to provide the plants with moderate watering. Make sure that you evenly the root part only and not the head.

Starting

Location: You will need to provide conditions of full sun. You can allow some shade, but in that case, the growth will be slow.

Planting: Broccoli can grow the best in temperatures ranging between 65 degrees Fahrenheit and 72 degrees Fahrenheit. You can sow them outdoors when the temperature of the soil is forty degrees Fahrenheit or lower.

Growing

Broccoli plants can deal with frost very well. As the system of roots is shallow, you will need to use mulch for better growth.

Harvesting: In case you see flowers of yellow color, you will need to harvest the heads immediately. You will have to consume them as soon as possible. You can harvest the center part of each plant with the use of shears for encouraging side shoot growth.

Problems: The most common problem is aphids. You will need to use strong water spray for removing them. If needed, use row covers.

Beet

Scientific name: Beta vulgaris

Details: You can consume beet roots and greens. They can be pickled, roasted, boiled, or grilled for consumption. In case you want to freeze them, you can do that as well.

Family: Chenopodiaceae

Season of growing: In case you are living in a warm climate, you can grow beet during late fall or early spring. If you live in a cold climate, you can

Zone: Three through ten

Spacing: Twelve inches apart

Seed harvesting: Forty to sixty days

Seed starting (indoor): Not suggested

Outdoor planting (earliest): During cool weather, in early spring, when you can work on the garden. In areas where there is no risk of frost, you can sow during fall.

Watering: One-inch water every week

Starting

Location: Conditions of full sun is recommended. You can also grow beet in partial shade.

Planting: Beets cannot be grown in soil that is acidic in nature. The preferred pH level is between six and seven.

Growing

When excessive nitrogen is provided, the top part can grow much better in comparison to the roots.

Harvesting: You can harvest the greens when the height is about five inches. The roots can be harvested when they are about three inches in total diameter.

Problems: Leaf miner is a common problem. You will need to destroy all the affected leaves.

Carrot

Scientific name: Daucus carrot

Details: You can plant carrots after certain weeks for a getting continuous harvest.

Family: Apiaceae

Season of growing: You can grow carrots during fall and spring, relying on your location. You will need to check the zones for the proper time.

Zone: Three through ten

Spacing: Three to five inches apart planted in rows that are two feet apart.

Seed harvesting: Sixty to eighty days

Seed starting (indoor): You can plant them in the garden soil directly as it is better not to transplant them.

Outdoor planting (earliest): Right after the danger of frost is cleared. In areas that are free from frost, you can plant them during fall.

Watering: You will need to keep the plants moist but not at all saturated. You can opt for drip irrigation for the best results.

Starting

Location: Full sun is recommended

Planting: You will need to cover the seeds with one-inch soil after sowing. It is better to sow them in deep and loose soil for better growth of the root system.

Growing

You will need to take care of watering and weeding only. You cannot grow carrots in clayey soil.

Harvesting: Just twist the top part and pull out the roots. Make sure that you do not break the top part. Cut the tops for storage.

Problems: One of the most common problems is aster yellow disease. This disease can result in short tops and roots with hair. You can use sticky traps for keeping the pest away from the plants. Another problem is fusarium. It can result in the rotting of roots when the carrots are in the ground right before the time of harvesting.

Cilantro

Scientific name: Coriandrum sativum

Details: You can harvest them as cilantro (fresh herb) or as coriander seed. For getting cilantro, you will need to harvest once the leaves appear right before flowering. For getting coriander, you will need to harvest the seeds after they are grayish-brown in color.

Family: Apiaceae

Season of growing: During early summer and spring

Zone: Three through ten

Spacing: Eleven to fifteen inches

Seed harvesting: Seventy to ninety days

Seed starting (indoor): Seven to eight weeks before the last frost

Outdoor planting (earliest): Right after frost danger

Watering: Cilantro will need one-inch water every week

Starting

Location: Conditions of full sun are recommended

Planting: Cover the seeds with a light layer of soil. You can plant after three weeks continuously for a steady harvest.

Growing

There is no need to provide fertilizer to the plants.

Harvesting: You will need to cut the greens at two inches from the ground.

Problems: The primary problem is wilting. You will need to water the plants properly for preventing this.

Chives

Scientific name: Allium schoenoprasum

Details: They can act as a good focal point in the garden and can also be used for various cuisines.

Family: Amaryllidaceae

Season of growing: During late spring

Zone: Three through ten

Spacing: Four to five inches apart

Seed harvesting: Eighty to ninety days

Seed starting (indoor): Nine to ten weeks before the last frost of spring

Outdoor planting (earliest): After the heavy frosting danger

Watering: You will need to water the seedlings properly right after planting. The plants will need one inch of water every week.

Starting

Location: Conditions of full sun is required

Planting: The seeds need to be covered with half-inch soil

Growing
The only maintenance that is required is watering and weeding.

Harvesting: You will need to clip the plants one inch above the level of the ground. The top portion will regrow.

Problems: There is no problem as such.

Corn

Scientific name: Zea mays

Details: You will need to keep the various varieties away from each other for preventing cross-pollination. It can also affect the quality and flavor of the corn after harvesting.

Family: Poaceae

Season of growing: During late spring

Zone: Three through ten

Spacing: Five to seven inches in straight rows at three inches apart

Seed harvesting: Eighty to ninety days

Seed starting (indoor): You can sow them directly in the garden soil.

Outdoor planting (earliest): Right after frost

Watering: The plants will need one to two inches of water every week during the cycle of growth. You can opt for drip or hose irrigation for the best results.

Starting

Location: Condition of full sun is needed for proper growth.

Planting: You will need to cover the seeds with a soil layer of one inch after sowing. Mix fertilizer of slow-releasing character in the soil before planting. You can follow the directions on the label for proper usage and mixing.

Growing

The only required maintenance is watering and weeding.

Harvesting: Each stalk of corn plant can produce two corn ears. But, if you for the hybrid varieties, you can get more yield. The perfect time of harvesting is when the silk ends of the ears dry out and are brown in color. You can pinch your nails in corn kernels for checking whether they are firm or not. You might even need to pull out the corn husk a bit for checking the condition of the produce. Give a small twist to the corn ear, and a firm tug is enough for releasing the same.

Problems: The primary problem of corn is corn earworm. Such pests can be found at the end part of the corn ears. You will need to trim and remove the corn ends. You can also use mineral oil of food-grade quality in the corn ear ends as the silk changes its color to brown. Mild insecticide can be used for dealing with pests as well.

Onion

Scientific name: Allium cepa

Details: You can harvest onions in the form of green onion or as onion bulbs when full maturity is allowed.

Family: Amaryllidaceae

Season of growing: Depending on the growing location, onion can be grown in spring and during fall. You can check the zones for the proper time.

Zones: Three through ten

Spacing: Three to five inches apart in straight rows that are one feet part

Seed harvesting: If you are planting seeds, it will take 120 to 140 days. If you are planting for green onion, it will take 70 to 100 days. For getting onion bulbs, it will take 90 to 120 days.

Seed starting (indoor): Seven to ten weeks prior to the last frost of spring

Outdoor planting (earliest): After the danger of frost

Watering: You will need to keep the root area and the tops dry. Watering the plants with drip or ditch irrigation is recommended.

Starting

Location: Conditions of full sun is needed

Planting: You will need to plant the sets of onion by covering the white part. Cover the seeds with half-inch soil after sowing.

Growing

As onions come with a shallow system of roots, you will need to provide them with enough water most of the time. Try not to make the top part wet.

Harvesting: You can harvest bulbs of onion as the tops start turning yellow in color. Bend the tops and pull out the bulbs.

Problems: Onions are not much prone to pests.

Gardening Resources

- American Hemerocallis Society: www.daylillies.org

- United States Department Of Agriculture: www.usda.gov.in

- American Hosta Society: www.americanhostasociety.org

- Perennial Plant Association: www.perennialplant.org

- Royal Horticultural Society: www.rhs.org.uk

CHAPTER 5

List Of Common Gardening Terms

There are certain gardening terms that you will need to know before you opt for the world of gardening. Let's have a look at them.

- **Annuals:** Variety of plants that tend to complete their cycle of life within one year or even less than that. Annual varieties of crops can produce profusely for a long period.

- **Biennials:** Both vegetables and flowers that tend to complete their cycle of life within two years. They tend to show the growth of leaves in the first year and produce fruits and flowers in the next.

- **Baby greens:** Leafy herbs and green veggies that are harvested when they are 2 – 4 inches tall.

- **Bolting:** The condition of early flowering in edible type crops that result in non-tasty plants.

- **Burpless cucumbers:** Cucumber variety that does not produce a chemical known as cucurbitacin. This chemical is bitter in taste and can result in slight indigestion.

- **Cold climate:** Freezing temperatures, typically USDA zones ten and even cooler.

- **Companion planting:** Growing different types of plants together that can benefit from each other. For instance, growing plants that can attract pollinators right next to plants that need pollination.

- **Compost:** Organic matter that is made from decomposed materials of plants. It is used for replenishing the nutrients of the soil and for reducing landfill waste.

- **Cover crop:** Plants that can grow fast, such as legumes, grains, or grass, that are used for one or even more than one quality of enhancing the soil quality. Such crops are removed from the garden before they start producing seeds.

- **Crop:** Plants that are grown for harvest, such as vegetables and cutting flowers.

- **Days to emerge:** The total number of days, on average, that will be taken by a seedling for emerging from the soil surface or from the medium under favorable conditions.

- **Days to harvest:** The total number of days from sowing of seeds to harvesting.

- **Deadheading:** Cutting off spent flowers from plants for encouraging blooming again. It is done for extending the period of blooming.

- **Direct sow:** Sowing plant seeds directly in the soil or in the permanent space of growing.

- **Disease resistance:** Exhibiting immunity or less susceptibility against certain diseases in comparison to others.

- **Disease tolerance:** Better ability to thrive with infection stress in comparison to others.

- **Drought tolerance:** Capability of thriving or surviving in conditions of low water. They are also called 'water-wise.'

- **Etiolation:** Having characteristics of weak, lanky, pale growth of plants that results from conditions of low light, or no light.

- **Fairly tolerant to drought:** Capability of surviving or thriving in conditions of low water, but to a fairly less extent than drought-tolerant plants.

- **Frost tolerant crop:** Crops that can tolerate frost and cold weather. The tolerance amount will vary from one plant to the other.

- **Frost sensitive crop:** Crops that cannot tolerate cold weather or frost. Such types of crops can die from freezing temperatures.

- **Fruit:** Capsule of seed that results from flowers, for example, melon and tomato.

- **Full sun:** Having sunlight for six hours or more than that.

- **Germination:** The time when seeds start growing.

- **GMO:** Genetically Modified Organisms. They are engineered genetically, which indicates that the concerned variety has been manipulated at the genetic level in the laboratory.

- **Gynoecious:** Plant that produces flowers for accepting pollens. A plant of pollinator type with flowers that can produce pollen is needed for producing fruits. They can mature very fast and are productive in nature.

- **Hardening off:** The one week to ten days process of acclimatization of plants that started indoors for adapting to outdoor conditions.

- **Heat tolerance:** The capability of resisting issues that are triggered by heat such as bitterness, poor pollination, lacking fruit set, premature flowering, etc.

- **Hybrid:** Two varieties of parent crops are bred for achieving hybrid offspring of the first generation.

- **Indeterminate:** Varieties of tomato that can produce and grow tomatoes all throughout the season until the very first frost.

- **Medium:** Used for the purpose of horticulture, it is the material in which plants are grown.

- **Microgreen:** Leafy, young veggies, and herbs that are usually harvested above the line of soil as the plants develop the cotyledons.

- **Mild climate:** Temperature that is not freezing in nature. USDA zones ten and even warmer can be included in this.

- **Monoecious:** Types of plants that can grow both pollen-receiving and pollen-growing parts.

- **Native:** The plants that originate from a particular zone or place in the world.

- **Organic seed:** Seeds that are grown in organic properties. Guidelines of USDA are followed in regard to the quality of soil, weed control, and pest. Fertilizer uses are also controlled according to the guidelines.

- **Open-pollinated:** Variety of plants that produce seeds that are of true nature, developing into identical types of plants.

- **Part shade/part sun:** Receiving sunlight for a period of 3 – 6 continuously.

- **Perennials:** Types of plants that can live for two years or more than that.

- **Pollination:** Fertilization of flower by insect, wind, birds, etc. The male pollen will reach the female stigma that will produce seeds.

- **Pollinator:** Organism that helps in transferring pollens.

- **Row cover:** Fabric that is used for keeping out pests and also for maintaining the optimal temperature. They are also used for protecting the plants from rain, strong wind, frost, and others.

- **Scarification:** The process in which the outer covering of the seed breaks for permitting moisture inside.

- **Sprout:** Type of germinated seed that is not grown in any kind of medium but is rinsed in plain water several times every day.

- **Thinning:** The process of reducing excess seedlings for providing proper spacing for the plants.

- **Transplanting:** The act of transferring small plants from one place to the other.

- **Vernalization:** Type of cold treatment that helps in inducing flowering in certain varieties.

CHAPTER 6

Companion Planting Guide

Plants require good friends to thrive. Except for the concept of fruiting and growth, plants are idle in nature. Most plants are planted in one spot and do not seem to have any form of control over the environment of growth. But, the relationships between plants are of varied nature, more or less like human relationships. In the communities of plants, there are certain plants that can provide each other with the required support. But, some plants cannot just get along. Just like human beings, plants also compete for space, nutrients, and resources.

Certain types of plants tend to grow rapidly and crowd others. Such plants also take away more of their share of sun, nutrients, and water. Some plants also give out toxins that can disturb the growth of plants and can even kill them. A very common example is the tree of black walnut that produces a toxin named hydrojuglone. Other plants act as the upstanding citizens and help others by providing nutrients to the growing soil and attracting important insects to the plants. They can even help by confusing the other insects that are searching for the host plants.

As an efficient gardener, you will need to be the city planner and mayor of the garden city. When you grow plants with a good set of companions, you can bring prosperity and peace to your town. On the other hand, growing plants of disruptive nature can ruin the garden. As with the planning of your garden city, the manner in which you will be laying out the garden of vegetables is very crucial. Try to avoid as much as you can to plant veggies in huge patches or even long rows. You can opt for interplanting vegetables with herbs and flowers. If you group one type of vegetable in a large area, it can easily attract problematic pests. When you opt for mixing herbs and flowers with the vegetables, pests will find it difficult to find the host plants. The scent of herbs and flowers, and also the color can confuse various pests. Certain herbs and flowers can also attract useful insects to the garden.

The habit of growth is not the only characteristic that you will need to consider while companion planting. You will need to be properly aware of the nutritional requirements of the plants as well. As you grow plants together that need a similar type of nutrients, the plants are most likely to compete for the resources. This can result in slowing the speed of growth of the plants. That is why it is recommended to grow plants that come with comes with complementary needs of nutrients.

Companion planting can very well mimic the characteristics of nature. When you grow crops that can complement each other naturally, several problems related to conventional farming can be avoided with ease. All that you will get is a healthy garden that can provide you with high yields. It will be easier for you to maintain a garden of this kind.

Three Sisters

One of the oldest examples of companion planting is Three Sister Planting. It is the growing trio of beans, winter squash, and corn. These three plants were typically grown together by the communities of Native America because of the complementary nature of the plants. The corn plant can grow tall that can support the climbing beans, and the squash will grow low. It can provide shade to the soil area with the big leaves and can also help in discouraging pests and weeds. The growth of beans can supplement the soil with nitrogen.

Now corn, beans, and squash are not the only group of plants that can establish a relationship of this kind. There are various other combinations. You can combine a wide variation of fast-growing crops with the slow-growing ones, aromatic and edible herbs, nitrogen fixers, and stacking plants. This will help you to easily double the possibility of increasing the annual yield for your garden. As an extra benefit, you can grow a crop of alfalfa, white clover, or other nitrogen fixers during the off-season. In this way, you will be able to restore the essential nutrients in the soil. This can guarantee you more harvesting sessions with more percentage of yields.

Let us have a look at some of the most common combinations of growing plants.

Companion Planting Chart

Plants	Companions	Allies	Enemies
Asparagus	Parsley, basil, tomato	Pot marigold can be used for deterring beetles	
Beet	Cabbage family, bush beans, onion, lettuce	Garlic can help in improving flavor and growth	Beet and pole beans can reduce the growth of each other
Beans	Cabbage family, beet (for bush variety only), celery, carrot, cucumber, eggplant, chard, corn, radish, potato, strawberry	Marigold can keep away Mexican beetles. Rosemary and nasturtium can also help in deterring bean beetles. They can be used for improving flavor and growth	Onion, garlic, and shallot can stunt the overall growth of beans
Carrot	Lettuce, beans, pepper, pea, onion, tomato, radish	Chives can improve flavor and growth. Sage and rosemary can be	Dill will slow down growth.

		used for deterring carrot fly.	
Chard	Cabbage family, beans, onion		
Celery	Cabbage family, beans, tomato	Garlic and chives can deter aphids. Nasturtium can help in deterring aphids and bugs	
Cucumber	Cabbage family, beans, pea, corn, tomato, radish	Marigold can be grown for deterring beetles. Nasturtium can deter bugs, beetles, and aphids. It can also help in improving flavor and growth. Tansy can deter beetles, ants, flying insects, and bugs. Oregano can deal with pests.	Sage is not at all for the health of cucumber plants

Corn	Cucumber, beans, melon, pea, parsley, squash, potato, pumpkin	White geranium and odorless marigold can easily prevent Japanese beetles. Pigweed can raise important nutrients from the layer of subsoil so that they are accessible to the corn plants.	Corn and tomato are prone to the same nature of worms.
Lettuce	Cabbage family, beet, onion, carrot, strawberry, radish	Garlic and chives can deter aphids	
Eggplant	Pepper and beans	Marigold can deter nematodes	
Melon	Pumpkin, squash, corn, radish	Marigold can help in deterring beetles. Oregano can provide protection from general pests.	

		Nasturtium can deter beetles and bugs	
Parsley	Corn, tomato, asparagus		
Onion	Cabbage family, beet, carrot, lettuce, chard, pepper, tomato, strawberry	Summer savory and chamomile can help in improving the flavor and growth. Pigweed can raise important nutrients from the layer of subsoil so that they are accessible to the onion plants.	Growth of beans and pea can be stunted by onion
Pepper	Eggplant, carrot, tomato, onion		
Pea	Carrot, beans, corn, turnip, radish, cucumber	Mint can help in improving the flavor and health. Chives can be	Growth of peas can be stunted by onion and garlic

		helpful for deterring aphids	
Pumpkin	Melon, corn, squash	Marigold can help in deterring beetles. Oregano can provide protection from general pests. Nasturtium can deter beetles and bugs.	
Potato	Cabbage family, beans, corn, pea, eggplant	General protection can be provided to potato by planting horseradish by the corners of a patch of potato. Marigold can help in deterring beetles.	Potato and tomato are prone to be attacked by similar blight.
Tomato	Carrot, asparagus, celery, parsley,	Bee balm, mint, and chives can help in improving	Tomato and corn are prone to the same worms.

	cucumber, pepper, onion	flavor and health. Basil can repel mosquitoes and flies.	Potato and tomato are prone to be attacked by similar blight.

CONCLUSION

Thank you for making it through to the end of *The Beginner's Vegetable Garden 2021*. Let's hope it was informative and was able to provide you with all of the tools you need to achieve your goals, whatever they may be.

Now your job is to plan a proper way of setting up a vegetable garden on your own. With the help of the various types of gardening, setting up a garden is not a tough job today. You can opt for the gardening type by relying on your needs and space. If you are willing to grow something on your own, having a vegetable garden as a beginner will be a great choice. Just concentrate on your goal, and you will be able to adapt to the growing system very easily. Make sure that you opt for companion planting for improving the flavor, growth, and health of the plants. Gardening is not that tough. All that you will need to do is spend some time nurturing the knowledge that you have received from this book and put the same into use.

In case you are not sure about the types of plants that you should plant, you can get help from the companion planting guide. As a beginner, it might feel a bit tough to manage disease and pests in the garden. But, with time and practice, you will soon be the master of your own garden.

Finally, if you found this book useful in any way, a review on Amazon is always appreciated!

CPSIA information can be obtained
at www.ICGtesting.com
Printed in the USA
LVHW100954211120
672149LV00008B/239